HOW TO GET YOUR BOOK PUBLISHED

HOW TO GET YOUR BOOK PUBLISHED

*A Practical Guide to authorship
and publishing*

GERALD SPARROW

Bachman & Turner Ltd
London

© Gerald Sparrow 1980

First published 1980
by
Bachman & Turner Ltd
The Old Hop Exchange
1/3 Central Buildings
Southwark Street
London SE1

ISBN 0 85974 089 7 Hardcover
     0 85974 094 3 Limp edition

Typeset by Inforum Ltd., Portsmouth
Printed in Great Britain by
The Camelot Press Ltd, Southampton

Contents

Author to Reader

This book is intended to be a practical handbook which tells the new author all he needs to know before starting his first book.

I submit my credentials first.

I retired from the law at the age of fifty-two. For the last twenty years I have been a professional author earning a sufficient income for myself and my family by writing forty books published by top publishers in Britain and the U.S.A. It has been an enjoyable and varied second career.

With my wife I have visited twenty-four countries as guest of the Authorities concerned with Tourism, usually a Ministry or Department of the host Government. My other "lines" have been Crime and the Far East. I have also done autobiography and biography. In short, I have cashed in on an interesting life.

Because of this I have not hesitated to quote personal experience in this book, if by doing so I could make the solution of difficulties easier or the necessity of adopting certain techniques clearer.

The young man or woman setting out on a career of authorship lacks the advantage of experience but more than compensates for this by being very much part and parcel of current young society with its constantly changing patterns. You can start in the book writing business at any age.

When I took the plunge I could find no book that told me comprehensively and succinctly how to become a viable author. Yet, like all other jobs, it has its rules, its hazards and its tricks of the trade. I had to learn how to do it the hard way by experience, by making mistakes, by attempting to rectify them.

A book such as this one would have saved me so much wasted time and frustration. I hope that it may do just that for you.

Gerald Sparrow
Brighton 1979

CHAPTER 1

Starting Out — Choosing your Line

If you will read this book from beginning to end you will be in a position to start a career as a writer of books, earning an income which will reflect your determination and your talent.

Let us define our aim.

By "viable" we mean making a living. By "author" we mean writing books as opposed to journalism. There is no hard line that separates the amateur author from the professional. Most authors start as amateurs and, attracted by the author's life, later become professionals which usually means they have contractual relations with a particular publisher, achieve a certain level of sales with regularity, and devote either their whole working time, or a fair portion of it, to the writing business. The author's essential occupation is writing books and the books he may write, as we shall see, divide themselves into several categories. The choice of the right kind of book for you is the secret of starting a writing career on the right path.

Let us take the young man of twenty-five attracted to writing as a career and not seeking a press appointment. He does not wish to be employed. He wants to be self-employed. Writing and literature have probably attracted and even absorbed him for years. He is prepared to face and overcome the hazards of embarking on a literary career, backing his own talent and industry to come through the early rough passage, together with some frustration, and much hard work, in order to win a position among recognised authors in Britain or the United States or wherever his home is.

If his home is in the city of New York or in London he starts with one advantage. The world book market is dominated by London and New York. Between them they effectively cover the world. The advantage of living near either of these capitals is considerable, because man-to-man contact with agents and publishers is easier. But if you live in Liverpool or Boston, or further afield, the disadvantage can be overcome and

1

has been overcome by many good and established writers.

The young writer has usually not had the advantage of a full and long experience at home and abroad, but he has the great advantage of being very much a part of the current scene with its accent on youth and progress. I have always held the view that men and women in their twenties, thirties, or early forties make the best novelists. The reason is not far to seek. They are impressionable. They have a vivid and clear imagination. They are willing to defy conventional codes of faith and morality. They combine a fresh idealism with a pragmatic approach that cuts through humbug and pomposity. A young writer, sufficiently daring, and with some talent, can explode on to the literary scene and score an instant success. Then follows the more difficult task of making his second book as good as his first and even of promoting a cult and an image that will secure him a following of readers who greet each new book with enthusiasm. Provided he is not spoilt by success, and continues to work hard and carefully and to base his books on accurate research, for him the sky is the limit and he has a real chance of reaching a recognised position as a national and international author.

Let us take the other extreme, the man in his late fifties who, on retirement, finds that he needs an occupation that will not only bring in an income but keep him vigorous and active in mind and body. Authorship is by no means beyond him. He will not have the young man's daring and uninhibited challenge. To some extent the years of work either in a profession or business, as an employer or employee, will have left him with ideas he finds it difficult to change and an attitude to life which has become part of his character and thinking.

The middle-aged or elderly man may, however, have one rich well on which he can draw for his books. A long and sometimes exciting experience of men, women and life in peace and war, in affluence and sometimes in danger and dire need. Out of these experiences he can take the material for his books and they will be in the category of factual books, or what is known as "faction", that is books based on fact but given a gloss by the writer's expertise and method of presentation. These books differ basically from the novel which is fiction.

May I illustrate the opportunities that the retired man may

have by telling you exactly what happened to me? I retired from the law at the age of fifty-two. Most of my working life had been spent up to this time as a Legal Adviser in the Ministry of Justice, Bangkok, sitting as a Judge in the Extra-territorial Court dealing with British subjects — Malays, Indians and Europeans resident in Siam (now Thailand). From December 8th, 1941 to 1945 I was a prisoner of the Japanese in Bangkok. On my liberation (by General Slim) I practised law successfully in Bangkok until returning to England for good in 1954. This life provided me with a fairly wide knowledge of murder, opium, glamorous and attractive women of many nationalities, absolute monarchy, revolution, gangsters, imprisonment as well as an indulgent and happy life in a bewitching country.

On returning to London I took a holiday in Budleigh Salterton — a small town in Devonshire with an excellent golf course. After three weeks, though I found the retired community kind and civilised, I got bored and wrote my first book, *Land of the Moonflower*, the story of my life in Siam. Since then I have written and had published two books a year on the following subjects: popular crime (fact); stories of the hot countries of South-East Asia (faction); and "magnet" books on tourism, promoting the tourist image of a particular country. In a later chapter we will explore these fields more minutely but here I want to show that the older author can link what he writes to the life he has lived. He may depart from this routine. I wrote six radio plays, one television play, one book of short stories and three biographies — but always returned to the well of experience for my regular books.

I was lucky to have survived an exciting and at times a dangerous life, but most men — even those engaged in seemingly prosaic business — have experienced events and hazards that, on looking back, are bizarre and intrinsically interesting. The stuff of which good strong narrative may be made. Good writing is very much concerned with the hearts as well as the heads of men and women, and people are so individual, react so strangely and unpredictably to certain pressures, that the book of the year may well be written by a man or woman employed all their lives in a spinning factory. The drama and the vitality, the passion and the dreams may all be there and with talent and honesty such a person can write a book which deserves and achieves success and critical as well as popular appreciation.

The truth is that wherever a man or woman lives, whatever their trade or profession, whatever their lives have been, in their experience — sometimes deep down — there is a story and if that story is told with freshness and sincerity it has a chance of making a good book.

So the writer setting out to become an author has to choose his "line". No one can choose it for him, but at least certain guide-lines may help him to make the right decision.

1. The types of literature open to the writer are numerous. Autobiography, biography, the novel, space-fiction, the short story, the historical novel, crime both by way of fact and faction as well as fiction. Travel and tourism (which are distinct from one another). Television plays, radio plays, plays for the live theatre. Technical and educational books. All are examples of the diversity of opportunity, each demanding a different approach, diverse research, special skills, and aimed at their own market. But the new writer will discover one or more for which he has some special aptitude. To make a choice will not be difficult. To make the right choice may be more difficult. If at first you make a wrong choice, change course. This is one of the most important decisions you will have to make in your writing career.

2. Review your experiences and your enthusiasm and then ask yourself the question: What am I suited to write? And then: What would I like to write?

3. Write a synopsis of about 2,000 words outlining a book in the category and on the subject you have in mind and see if it comes easily or with difficulty. Check whether it is logical, having a beginning, a middle and an end as well as continuity and makes a satisfying whole.

4. Approach the synopsis without inhibitions. Stick firmly to the category you have chosen. If you find you can write this short synopsis, divide it into say fifteen chapter headings and remember that this would be the embryo of a book of 60,000 to 70,000 words.

Try yourself out on the nursery slopes before you risk the big run. You will find it an intriguing exercise in itself and, if you repeat it with a different subject, you will soon realise what comes easily and naturally and what, for some reason, is not your line.

Difficulties often arise for new writers because, having conceived an idea for a book, they charge straight away into

4

Chapter One, page one, without the very necessary exercise of the synopsis. They have the feeling— and it is a natural one — that their inspiration will carry them through. But the result may be a chaotic piece of work. If you have done this, do not, in disappointment, throw it away. Never throw anything away. There may be in it paragraphs which you will never write better. It may contain dialogue that you can use in your next effort after you have gone through the discipline of the synopsis.

The synopsis must contain the whole story and nothing else. It is an abbreviated miniature of your whole book.

I cannot stress too much the usefulness of the synopsis technique which will provide you, not only with an early warning as to whether you are on the wrong lines, but also encouragement if you have chosen correctly. For very little labour it will bring you a bonus of useful information and a clear guide line.

If you have completed say three resumés on different subjects, you will almost certainly be able to say: That's the one that vibrates. That's the one that came easily. If this happens then that is the right one. The temptation at this point is to surge forward into a manuscript.

But what about the research? The deeper you dig the better the crop. Suppose your story has a background of actors in London or New York. You must know not only the kind of lives that typical stage people lead, their work, their superstitions, their contracts, their scripts, their sex life and their hobbies in general, but be sufficiently familiar with their world to recreate its feeling, its tensions, its temptations, its disappointments and its triumphs.

If you are writing of the sea, then the salt must impregnate your pages. The ugliness as well as the kind countenance of the ocean must all be there. If you are writing of professional people, you must research to an extent that makes you dead accurate in every detail. If possible, live with your material for a time. It constantly astounds me how many competent television writers get lawyers, both barristers and solicitors, wrong. And the same may be said of politicians though not to the same extent.

So the real place for research is on location with the people you are intending to write about.

Whether you are writing fact or fiction, dates are important and all that dates dictate. Dates fix not only the year and month but also the decade and each decade has an atmosphere all its own. The Eighteen-nineties were the years of imperial splendour when it was true to say that the people of England had not spoken yet. The Edwardian age was the last glow of the "country house", the great ducal families, the master and servant relationship in industry. The First World War was a thing apart as a result of which the old order was shattered. The 'Twenties were a desperate, abandoned attempt to seize pleasure, put Humpty Dumpty together again. The 'Thirties were ominous. And so it went on.

No time spent on research is ever wasted. It does require perusing the bibliography and even the geography of your subject in public or private libraries but, as I have suggested, it may also include some weeks of practical research that may be just as valuable.

These suggestions apply largely to the scenery, the setting, and the atmosphere. When it comes to characters in fiction you must know them very well indeed. It is said that a good author sleeps, mentally at least, with his "heroine". He knows her on waking, he knows her in love, out of love, in tantrums and in genuine distress. Almost certainly the character will be based on someone he knows. At this stage the author does not have to be careful. Much later your manuscript will almost certainly be read for defamation — libel. I am including guide-lines on this subject in a later chapter. Do not hesitate to include characters based on friends and relations. So good is the opinion that most people have of themselves that they are unlikely to identify their portraiture and, if they do, they may well be flattered. After all, it is not every woman who can say, "Yes, I was Lavinia. Of course, he has not got me quite right ...."

My own experience is that whereas in writing it is essential to have the discipline of set hours, preferably in the morning, research can be done at any time that is convenient provided that when you are doing it you are not distracted but wholly absorbed in the work in hand. Notes on the research done are pure gold and must be filed immediately on your return to base. When you have completed your research, you will find that your notes contain not only the minimum of essential information but a great deal of the "trimmings" that help with atmosphere.

To sum up: You can start writing books at any age. The ploy of the synopsis will be a great help to you in deciding what your line of literature should be and save you much time and possible error. And, as soon as you have a good synopsis of a book that pleases you critically, then start your research so that the critics will never be able to say that you do not know your subject.

When this period of preparation is over you will be ready to settle down to your manuscript. But before you do so, let me introduce you to the tools of your trade.

CHAPTER 2

The Tools of the Trade

Authors have never agreed on the best way to write a manuscript. Some prefer to type the MS themselves. For this exercise it is not necessary to be a "typist" in the modern sense. Two fingers are all that is needed for they perform at a pace that can follow the invention of the brain. Expert typing and the most modern typewriters geared to high performances are not for this job.

A few authors find that they prefer to dictate to a secretary, and if she is pleasing, experienced, and understanding, this may prove a speedy way to producing a manuscript that has been very well researched.

A number of writers swear that they can turn out good work by means of a dictaphone but most, I think, find this relentless little machine difficult to work with. After a break or pause one cannot obtain the last paragraph or line without a play back and this involvement in mechanics is idea-destroying.

Though each author will settle his exact method and routine of production for himself there would, I think, be general agreement on the necessary "tools of the trade".

First on the list must be the typewriter. A good second-hand typewriter, well maintained, and fed with the best ribbons, is a major must.

Next the dictionaries. The *Concise Oxford Dictionary* (Clarendon Press), a pocket dictionary, and an Anglo-French dictionary should be sufficient. The French dictionary is there in a supplementary capacity for it often gives a slant on the nuance of a phrase or individual words.

There are optional aid books which some authors are practically married to and others find helpful. Firstly, *Fowler's Modern English Usage. The Dictionary of Modern English Usage,* to give it its full title, is a long work running to 700 pages, and its purpose is to sort out current English speech and writing and make it concise and intelligible. There is a companion volume, *A Dictionary of Modern American Usage,* which is equally comprehensive and useful.

The *Concise Oxford Dictionary of Quotations* (Oxford University Press) is a delight. For example, instant Housman is there for the plucking. "The bells that sound on Bredon ...."

Finally, still optional, *Roget's Thesaurus.* Mine is a Penguin Reference Book. It is described as "The Thesaurus of English words and phrases, classified and arranged so as to facilitate the expression of ideas and to assist in literary composition." If I remember correctly the Greek word *thesauros* means treasure. That is what this book is.

None of the books I have mentioned is essential for the new writer, but all are useful. When we come to the Encyclopaedias then it is a different matter, for a good modern Encyclopaedia is essential. As they tend to be expensive new, a second-hand one at a sale will do very well. It will cost about a tenth of its new selling price, because Encyclopaedias depreciate in purchasing price — though not in real value — even faster than motor cars.

Now comes an acquisition that most authors would classify as optional, but I regard as an absolute necessity, at least for writers interested in the past and in the astounding changes that have taken place recently in nearly all countries. Let us take a remote and, these days, little known country — Burma. In my modern Encyclopaedia the description of Burma shows an inward-looking state governed dictatorially with its northern Provinces in more or less constant revolt. Foreign contacts are frowned on and the economy is dwindling. An unhappy and slightly absurd mixture of mismanagement and unenlightened leadership. And no glamour.

It was not always thus. I turn to my richly gilded Victorian (1885) *National Encyclopaedia.* The second paragraph is entitled "Growth of the Burmese Empire". This was an eighteenth century phenomenon, for at this time the King of Burma "acquired" Pegu, Moggoung, Tenasserim, Manipur, Chocar, Arakan and Assam. In the nineteenth century, of course, the British raj took it all away and, instead of replacing King Thibaw by a more enlightened prince, governed Burma as if it were a province of India with which it had no cultural, political or ethnic ties whatever. But until the 1880's there was still Upper Burma and in Mandalay King Thibaw

9

lolled on his Peacock Throne, the Lord of Life, occasionally talkative because the French had introduced him to champagne, but usually — and always on State occasions — transformed by assuming the expression of the Buddha, a serenity and apartness that only Eastern absolute monarchs seemed capable of portraying. In this nineteenth century description of Burma we glimpse the Queen Soupayalat, beautiful, but with the "adder" brow and head of her family, the Hlwot-dau which was the King's executive cabinet, and the "wong-yees", the Burmese version of cabinet ministers who could be seen by a crouching crowd as they passed through Mandalay on the way to and from the Palace, accompanied their lictors and guards.

I have introduced this picture of a remote land to show that the use of two encyclopaedias gives the author a sense of perspective and a knowledge that may be vital to him when applied not to remote countries but even to the industrialised Western nations. The same benefits can be reaped if we are researching people, or language, or customs, or religion, or farming, or war, or any of the manifold activities of ordinary people. So I would say that a century-old encyclopaedia is worth its weight in diamonds. I bought mine in excellent condition and in fifteen volumes for £1 twenty years ago. It would not cost more than £10 at a sale today.

Whittaker's Almanack is an absolute essential. It tells you annually everything you want to know about the current scene in the United Kingdom. The manifestos of the political parties are a free and a constant commentary on our society. Two newspapers, one slightly dull, snooty and lefty, but well written, like the *Guardian,* and one conservative like the *Daily Telegraph* (the only paper which reports bird migration with panache) and a Communist newspaper as well as a few National Front leaflets will keep you informed of the realities and absurdities of the political spectrum.

However reluctantly, one must keep in touch with the news of the day, for this is instant life when the newspaper is born at midnight and instant death next day, apart from its invaluable correspondence column, which sponsors debates and current happenings. The alert author can contribute if he needs some free publicity, but he will only have his "Letter to the Editor" accepted if it is first rate, to the point, reasonably brief, and well written.

There are minutiae of this "tools of the trade" business. Authors should not, I feel (shoot me if I am wrong), write with Biro pens. These are instruments for taking the character out of handwriting and even if you typewrite your letters to Publishers they can give you a zombie, soulless signature. A good fountain pen with a flexible nib is allowable and much better. A really expensive eraser rubber is essential. Top quality typing paper, preferably bought by the ream, good and durable carbon and a little paper gadget that enables you to delete words on carbon copies without making a mess. All these help and make your writing easier and more organised. Order and some simple filing system are really essential. I have achieved it, and if I can do it, anyone can do it ....

Perhaps the greatest help to good writing is great writing. Shakespeare, whoever he was, for drama and dialogue, is a beacon. Authors of our time can inspire lesser writers to write better. Consider this final epitaph on his father by Sir Winston Churchill at the end of his book on Lord Randolph, that brilliant but wayward politician.

> "There is an England that stretches far beyond the well-drilled masses who are assembled by Party machinery to salute with appropriate acclamation the utterances of their chosen fuglemen; an England of wise men who gaze without self-deception at the failings and follies of both political parties, of brave and earnest men who find in neither faction fair scope for the effort that is in them; of 'poor men' who increasingly doubt the sincerity of Party philanthropy. It was to that England that Lord Randolph Churchill appealed; it was that England he so nearly won; it is by that England he will be judged."

I was so struck with this that when I wrote a "poor man's" paperback life of Sir Winston in a successful attempt to make a Life of the national hero available to those who could not afford the many good but expensive biographies, I wrote the closing paragraph of the book called *Man of the Century"* as follows:

> "If God gave us memories so that we may have roses in December, Winston Churchill had memories that no man of his age could surpass. He typified in his person and in his character the finest attributes of both the British and the American peoples. We shall not see his

11

like again".

Mundane in comparison, redeemed perhaps by its sincerity.

All good books are the author's life line. He does not write alone. He is just one of a multitude who have gone before and will come after.

The collection of a private library is one of the most valuable aids to authorship. It should be collected slowly. Never buy in a hurry. All good second-hand books are sold for a pittance unless they have acquired some special value, so the gradual building up of a library will be a wonderful reservoir of good writing — and good reading. Because by now you have chosen the writing fields you intend to plough, a portion of the second-hand or even new books you buy will cover the subjects on which you intend to write yourself. Read these but never copy them. Use them to broaden your vision and total appreciation of your subject.

The public libraries are superlatively good both in Britain and in the United States and they are adequate in Europe. Make full use of them. The staff, when they know that an author is engaged in serious research, are always eager to help, but of course nothing can replace your own hard effort in the use of this great facility.

Most authors do not need solitude to write well. They do need a room, however, which for their working hours will give them privacy and no distractions. They are not, as a rule, beautiful people. They are workers, just as much as the Director in his Board Room or the man minding a machine for a weekly wage. Unfortunately, they do not present a united front to protect their interests and this has resulted in their betrayal by Parliament in the matter of lending rights. Solemn promises have been broken with cynical indifference. So the new author has to come to the book writing scene as he finds it. The verdict has to be that even now nothing will hold back talent supported by industry and integrity. At this early state as he is about to work on his first book, if he can afford it, the author would do well to join the Society of Authors. It is not perhaps the kind of ruthless pressure group that gets results, but it is the best representation we have and, as such, the main organised aid to the new author.

From the very beginning the author should, I think, realise that authorship is not only about writing and selling books.

He should know the difficulties that Publishers and Printers face in their business and a realisation of this will make his path easier and his relations happier.

So this is how a new author can set up in business. The investment should not exceed £200, and many, including myself, invested half that amount. For this investment he should be able, if he is dedicated and has some flair, to earn a fair income to keep himself and his family. There is no other self-employed profession for which the initial cost of equipment is so small and the rewards comparatively good. Nor need they end at the age of sixty-five, or seventy-five. You can work for as long as you want to work. Or you can "semi-retire" and confine yourself to writing one book a year when you feel that total activity in books, TV, radio and other sources of income, has become a burden.

Finally, at this stage, I suggest that the author who by definition is articulate has a duty to join in the great public debates of the day. He is in a unique position to do so. No man is his master. He is a man of ideas. He can sponsor unpopular causes that sin against transient fashion but are honest and right. This will lead later in his career to the author having a public image and attracting some publicity — not all of it flattering. The extension of his activities in this way will add greatly to the satisfaction he gains from having chosen the difficult but delightful profession of a man of letters.

This book is designed primarily to inform the new author on how to make a living but it will also outline the life of travel and diverse activity allied to properly exploited authorship.

CHAPTER 3

Writing the Manuscript

As this may be your first book, you will not be likely, unless you have a very special story to tell, to have it commissioned. Publishers do commission books before they are written but this is done as a rule to secure the contract for an outstanding book by a world figure, the "revelations" of a dictator, the autobiography of a famous or infamous woman, or even the story of someone whose position entails intimate contact with the golden light of a Throne, or an adventure that is in itself unique.

Apart from this, professional authors, with a reputation for delivering competent work on time are often commissioned by Publishers to ensure continuity of the Publisher-Author relationship and I had, over a period of years, a number of books commissioned on this basis after the synopsis had been submitted and approved. It was an arrangement convenient to both parties. It brought an immediate "advance" to the author and it enabled the Publisher to include the book in his List in good time and thus to secure advance publicity for it.

This kind of commissioning will not come to the new author unless he has fame or notoriety in another field. The new author, having chosen his line, must settle down, with no guarantee that his work will be saleable, to write a book of say seventy thousand words divided into perhaps three parts of twenty-five thousand words each, making fifteen chapters. It sounds a formidable task and in a sense it is, but it is not as daunting as it sounds provided you have by your side all that well selected and arranged research we have already discussed. And, of course, also on your desk you will have the synopsis which shows you exactly what you should include in Chapter 1 and, if the book is a novel, the way the story unfolds, the characters introduced into the opening sequences and the location and atmosphere of the initial and most important part of your story. There is no reason, if you can devote three hours a day to this task, why you should not finish your book in four to six months. Five thousand words is not too large an output for a week's work, if the research has been comprehensive and thorough.

Of course, there are authors who spend a year at least on a single book and others who live with a book for five years before they feel they can allow it to be born and dazzle the world. But we are considering the average writer whose drive impels him to write with despatch. How fast or how slow to go is dictated by the personality of the author, just as the pace of a horse in a jumping competition is often a balance between a clear round and the clock. The urgency of some writers, especially young writers, may be a positive advantage. By forcing the pace the whole story may sweep the reader along in excitement until the last page is written. However, the greater the pace, the more revision and correction will be necessary and this is of primary importance. If a book takes four months to write, it will benefit greatly by a month of minute revision.

If your book is fact, the same techniques apply but in this case you are not so much concerned with invention except in the comments that reflect the story as you see it.

Let me take an instance. I wrote two pieces on Horatio Bottomley whom I had only seen and heard once. It was at the Oxford Union while I was visiting. He started his speech with a Latin quotation that did not come off. Apparently the "quantities" were wrong. There was a titter. He paused, then said: "Gentlemen, I have not had your advantages. The only school I ever went to was the hard and sometimes bitter school of life...." He had them in his pocket.

Although both stories I wrote about him in *The Great Swindlers* and *The Great Defenders* were factual, much depended on bringing this extraordinary character alive. So I wrote this paragraph in a purely factual story. It was as important as the facts that followed:

"He was a portly, powerfully built little man with the face of a bulldog, a sensuous, agile face, a face alive with humour and mischief. The eyes showed the character of the man, for they missed nothing, they were quizzical, appraising eyes that weighed very quickly, and sent their message to the quick-silver brain that, for over a quarter of a century, had kept

Horatio Bottomley in great affluence, at the centre of affairs, a power in the City, the editor of *John Bull*, the Member of Parliament for Hackney."

And the drama at the end of his last trial, the first which led to a conviction for wide-scale fraud, though strictly factual, taken from the Court records, also needs the author's eye to make it come alive. I quote:

"Bottomley spoke for nearly two hours almost without notes. He was in turn derisive, humorous, compassionate, persuasive and appealing. He took the point that the prosecution were out to 'get him' regardless of the facts of the case. There was some substance in this. The Treasury certainly had been after him for years and, looking at prosecuting counsel in Court, those who were present felt that they had spared no effort to trap this man at last. After all it was their duty to do so and they did it.

"Bottomley's final speech ended, as usual, on a flood of emotion that appeared to be perfectly genuine, so that he could say things that for a lesser man would not have been possible. At the end of his speech he paused for a moment and appeared to be finished. Then he looked round once more to the jury and, leaning across towards them, raising his voice so that every word rang round the packed Court, he said:

"'Gentlemen, if any jury of Englishmen says that Horatio Bottomley is guilty of crimes such as these then that sword will fall from its scabbard.' As he said this he pointed to the sword of justice over the Judge's chair.

"Then he did a very clever thing. He had, he knew, to get back into the dock in order to hear the verdict of the jury and possibly to receive sentence. If he had hesitated he would have been led back by a policeman or by a warder or both. He was determined to avoid this. He took up his papers and bowed to the Judge with that extraordinary dignity he could assume at will and said to him: 'My Lord, I will now go to the place where accused persons always go.' He was remaining a free man to the very last."

I think this brings out an essential point in writing all manuscripts. The author, whether he is writing fact or fiction, must tell the story as he sees it. Unless he has generated some excitement in himself he is unlikely to move his readers. The whole art of telling a story — and the modern author is following in the wake of the professional story-teller of the

Eastern bazaar — is to say to the reader by implication — "Come with me, I have something to tell you and to show you that is interesting and wonderful." Taken by the hand, the reader follows. The rapport has to be established in the first chapter. The author, for the duration, is married to his manuscript. It will be the first thing he thinks of on waking and almost the last thing he thinks of before he sleeps. Women married to authors know this, so the wise married author masks the priority which the manuscript has in his life.

Tackling the manuscript involves the question of writing discipline. The morning is, for most of us, the best time for this task. From 6 a.m. to 9 a.m. is especially good because, as a rule, there is no interruption and no competition for your attention. For retired authors who have leisure, 9.30 a.m. to 12.30 p.m. makes a very good writing day. Some men can write at night. Most writers dissolve as the evening approaches, seduced by the temptations which darkness brings. Writing is for sobriety, for fresh ideas, for a lively, well-briefed, concentrated mind. You owe it to your manuscript to give it of your very best.

If you develop the technique of typing your own manuscript and correcting it yourself, either chapter by chapter — which I prefer — or on completion, and having the whole typed professionally thereafter, you do not need to type copies, but your typist will type an original and at least three copies. The original, of course, is for submission to your Publisher but the copies may well come in useful if, for instance, you are offering serial rights to a newspaper, or rights to a Publisher abroad. In both cases the purchaser knows that the original is with your Publisher so he has no objection to a copy being sent.

There is one other reason for having enough copies — security. Sir Harold Wilson gave me good advice on this point. Always have copies in at least three separate safe places. Sir Harold had been plagued with burglaries by thieves apparently after his papers. But it is sage advice even for those of us who are not likely to be the target of criminals. Do not write so fast that you have no time to refer constantly to your research notes and to be guided by your synopsis. The manuscript itself should be a genuine product of both the synopsis and the research. It should incorporate all the material you collected in your research and expand the story within the guide-lines of your synopsis. Done this way your progess should be orderly and coherent. It will be a case of steady-as-she-goes.

Do not be afraid of insertions either at the time of writing or during correction. Type them separately, indicating clearly where they start and where they end, when they take their place in the manuscript itself. These afterthoughts often add valuable information and even lustre to the story. When your typist comes to do the final original and copies take the time to go through each chapter with her, so that she understands each alteration and each addition and is able to amend the script accordingly. Nothing is more frustrating to a professional typist than confused directions on corrections, insertions or addenda. The author is the kingpin of the whole operation and he must work with his typist and later his Publisher and, in certain circumstances, with his Printer as well. Co-operation is all.

New authors often make their paragraphs too long for the readers' digestion. When you find yourself doing this seek the convenient break point and make two paragraphs of one. If you quote another author's work, remember that as a rule you must receive permission to do so.

"Changing gear", especially in novels and short stories (one of the most difficult forms of writing) is an art in itself. By "changing gear" we mean the point at which the author takes you from your inspection of the castle in Monaco to the Casino some hours later during a visit to the Principality in search of a wife who — apparently — has been abducted. A clumsy "change of gear" is off-putting and slightly ridiculous so you have to master this minor art and the best way I can think of to show you how it is done is to quote some examples of authors who have developed the trick to perfection. The apparent ease and simplicity mask a very professional mastery of this facet of narrative technique. The changes achieve their objective so unobtrusively that the reader is unshaken by the move in direction or even of location. The reader's attention is held completely.

The late Somerset Maugham did it as well as anyone ever has.

'What's Iwelei?' asked Mrs Macphail.

'The plague spot of Honolulu. The red light district.' Iwelei was on the edge of the city. You went down side streets....

One moment you are listening to a conversation. The next you are exploring the red light district of Honolulu, dank, dark and dirty, lightened only by its garish red lights.

He was at home. He was glad that he had been born in the most important city in the United States. Mr Hunter's automobile was waiting for them.

'Glad to be back, son?'

'I should just think I am,' said Bateman.

One moment, a young man's pride and excitement in arriving back in his home town, Chicago. The next, an easy transition to effortless dialogue that rings absolutely true.

It is not as easy as it looks. It comes with practice. It is the same art as that of the experienced advocate. It was said of Sir Edward Clarke, a great Victorian barrister, that he dealt with the difficulties of his cases as easily as a superb hunter sweeps over an easy fence. Inhibition is fatal to changing gear. It has to be natural — and quick — and clear. There must never be any doubt as to where the reader has been led to, and the transition must be so smooth that he hardly notices it, but completely understands it.

Many new writers find dialogue a problem. They can achieve good descriptive writing without difficulty but when it comes to dialogue they are apprehensive and falter. The cure for this is to listen with the closest attention to people talking. Do not join in the conversation. Just listen and learn. You will find that most sentences are short and sharp. Occasionally the speakers "interlock". Sometimes they both speak together, but normally they exchange short simple sentences that may not be grammatical but are quite clear. The meaning is not obscured unless there is an innuendo with a particular word or words used to contain an ulterior significance or message.

The art of dialogue actually consists of transporting live conversation onto the written page. Even so, the written version is apt to be a neatly trimmed account of the real thing. This does not really matter. Too exact a copy of real conversation might be tedious and involved, but the spirit and manner of it have to be reproduced. It should usually be casual and instantly understood. It is these qualities that have to be transmitted into the dialogue of a book. In order to achieve natural relaxed dialogue it is necessary for the writer to write without tension but with close attention. As soon as you have mastered the trick, the writing of dialogue is a delight. It breaks up the descriptive narrative and at its best reveals much more of character in fewer words.

A last example. Sir William Collins published my book, *The Green Garuda,* which had a success in America. The woman in my example had instructed me, as her lawyer, to start divorce proceedings against her husband who was still seeing his native mistress after his marriage to her. The story is set in Siam.

We had dined together on the last evening at her hotel. She told me that next day was her birthday.

She smiled. 'I shall be thirty-nine.'

'A good age.'

We said goodbye. I wished her luck. She thanked me for what I had been able to do.

'I'm afraid I've been an awful nuisance. Taking you away from other work. You see, I had to get it done quickly.'

'I understand. Goodbye.'

'Goodbye and thank you.'

Her plane left very early. It flew in from Hongkong at six and was off again in fifty minutes.

That morning I was immersed in a case that had engaged my attention for weeks. Three large contracts for rice shipments to Mombasa had broken down. It was intricate business. I did not notice that it was nearly two before I could leave for luncheon.

As I moved from my desk Nai Sumit opened my door and said:

'Mrs West, sir.'

I could not believe it. 'Why, did you miss your plane?'

'No. I did not go.'

'Why? I don't understand.'

Her face was hard no longer. Her eyes were shining.

'He loves me still. Today is my birthday. Do you know what he did? For three years he has given me a basket of orchids on my birthday. Last night he motored up from Singora — six hours — and left them, without a note, at the hotel. He's gone back.'

'And you?'

'I'm joining him on the afternoon train.'

'I shall have to wire to London.'

'Yes. You do understand, don't you?'

I understood.

In the writing business one is only occasionally at one's best. But perhaps this end to one story in a book of short stories is one with which I feel content. The motivation, the short descriptive passages, and the dialogue, seem to me to come easily and naturally. The only word which makes me pause is the word still. "He loves me still." Would she not in fact have said, "He still loves me."? One should avoid as a rule the temptation to be histrionic. The drama and the dialogue must at least seem to emerge inevitably from the story and not appear to be the manipulation of the author.

You will adopt rules and procedures of your own for writing your manuscripts. The methods suggested in this chapter are those that I have found effective and it was not until they became a part of the routine of my writing that I was able to achieve a professional book. But they can certainly be amended to suit your individual approach. Writers tend to be highly individualistic. The new writer, however, may well be able to formulate his own methods along the lines I have indicated, retaining his freedom of choice while benefiting by procedures found rewarding after years of trial and error.

CHAPTER 4

Publisher-Author Relationship

The more the author knows about his Publisher and his Publisher's business the better. Publishers are large and small, each has his own way of negotiating, each has books in which he specialises. Some Publishers are outside the ordinary run of the commercial publishing world. They specialise in religious books (the Bible, of course, is the world's best seller) or they concentrate on maps and guides, or on education, or some other specialised sphere of the wide range of books that annually find their way on to the market and for which there is a demand.

So how is the new author to get to know the facts about his prospective Publisher? The answer is the *Writers' and Artists' Year Book,* which is published each year by A & C Black, a firm founded in 1807 and maintaining the highest standard in the section of the publishing market they have made their own. The *Writers' and Artists' Year Book* will tell you the correct name of the publishing firm, its address and telephone number, the names (in most cases) of its directors and senior staff and, most importantly, the kind of books they specialise in. Although all the biggest publishing houses tend to have a general list and will list biography, belle-lettres, travel, fiction etc, many of the smaller publishing houses are more specialist than this and their specification of the kind of books they are prepared to publish is of vital importance to the new author.

Let us suppose that the position is that the new author knows nothing about his prospective Publisher and the Publisher knows nothing about the man or woman who has written the manuscript, which is one of perhaps fifty delivered through the post that week.

If the author will read carefully the announcements of each publisher under the heading United Kingdom Publishers, he will learn the essential facts he must know and he can choose a

Publisher who is at least interested in the type of book he has written and who will not be irritated by being sent a novel by an author who should have known that his firm does not publish fiction.

Then the other side of the picture. When a number of the Publishing staff or one of their "readers" opens the manuscript and starts to read, he is asking himself: "Is this book marketable? Is it intrinsically so good and exceptional that we can risk investing money in signing a contract with the author, printing, publishing selling at home and abroad, advertising and giving away complimentary copies as part of the promotion programme?" There is an old Banker's saying: "When in doubt, do nothing." And Publishers sometimes feel that there is much to be said for this attitude. They have to be convinced that the book is viable.

At this stage they have not met the author, but he can diminish such a handicap by enclosing a biographical note of himself, detailing briefly his background, his experience and his enthusiasms. Then both parties know something of each other and at their first meeting which, from the author's point of view, should be as soon as possible, they will know much more.

The more intrepid new authors manage to deliver their manuscripts themselves and to combine a first meeting with this move. It is not really fair to the Publisher because he has not had an opportunity of reading the manuscript or of having it read. So what other means are there of capturing the attention of the Publisher at this very early stage? Well, you can send a neatly typed copy of your synopsis attached to the manuscript, and it may well be that, as this is short, the Publisher will "dip into" this and if he likes what he reads he may even ask a member of his staff to read the MS instead of sending it to a reader.

The new author holds one more card up his sleeve — the blurb. The blurb is the brief description of the book that is usually printed on the inside of the cover-page. Perhaps I may give an example of my own. I only wrote one book of short stories, a very difficult market. The late Sir William Collins, whose courtesy and charm were quite exceptional, agreed to publish the book after I had sent him this "blurb".

These are stories of the new East and the Europeans and Americans who live there not as over-lords but as communities subject to local law as foreign residents.

Gerald Sparrow, living in Bangkok for twenty-four years and married to an Asian, knows the background of these remarkable stories intimately. The serenity, the intrigues, the sexuality, the occasional sudden violence, the captivating charm of the people and the unpredictable and swiftly moving pattern of uninhibited living lead the Europeans into situations which the author believes to be more compelling than the old static pattern of bygone days.

At the age of twenty-six, Gerald Sparrow was the youngest judicial appointment made from Britain to Siam in the days of the Absolute Monarchy.

He returned for good while still in the forties to become a professional writer, and lives in Brighton. He knows the East from many angles — as judge, lawyer, race-horse owner, restaurant proprietor, prisoner of the war years. He is not nostalgic and does not yearn for the stately, privileged past.

'I prefer the new East of today,' he says, 'to the East of yesterday. It is more dramatic, more real.'

These stories bear out this summing-up.

The point that is really made here is that the stories in my book are not in the tradition of Maugham. This is not the old East of privilege but the turbulent new East where the foreigner may well be a welcome guest, but he is subject to the laws of the country, has no special rights, and has to "operate" and secure his aims through the patronage of the Government in whose hands all power rests.

The book was called *The Green Garuda*. Largely through a most generous review by Professor Burt Harrison of Washington State University on Washington Radio and Television, and an approving word from the New York Times, *The Green Garuda* justified itself in the States as well as in the United Kingdom and overseas.

The invaluable *Writers' and Artists' Year Book* also gives the names and addresses of Commonwealth Publishers, American, Canadian and Australasian Publishers and South

24

African Publishers. If writing is to be your career, buy this book at once. You cannot do without it. It is the bible of the craft. It covers every facet of the writing business except that with which this book deals, that is how to write a viable book. It is essentially a reference book and a supremely good one, most carefully compiled.

The more the new author knows about his Publisher the better. It will enable him to appreciate his Publisher's problems. One of these may well be that a part of the book, or even a single chapter, is inappropriate, or for some reason objectionable and the Publisher knows that its inclusion would injure sales. If this happens, it is a cardinal error to cling tenaciously to the text as you have written it. I can only go back to personal experience and say, that in twenty years, all cuts, deletions, rewrites and alterations to my books in manuscript suggested by Publishers have improved the books. The reason is not far to seek. The Publisher does not wish to alter a manuscript. He only suggests it if his experience tells him that it is necessary. He will explain his reasons. Never regard what you have written as holy script. It is not. And you have a fine precedent for accepting suggestions. Shakespeare would alter the lines of a play if an actor said to him: "Master William, I cannot say that."

In this early stage of your relationship with your Publisher, if you are dealing with one man, it is essential to get his name and initials right. It may seem too unimportant a point to mention, but it is not. There is nothing more irritating than to have one's name mis-spelt. If the man — or woman — has any kind of degree or title that they like to have included in their address get that right too. Publishers like dealing with "civilised" authors and in their intensely competitive and sometimes cut-throat business good manners soften the asperities of daily life.

I stress a good and urbane approach because authors, being by nature highly individualistic, have been known to do strange things and behave in an odd way. One swashbuckling character — who had written a magnificent adventure story — accusing his publisher of dilatory payment, turned up in his office with a sword. Whether this pointed argument had the desired effect we do not know. Another young author, who was owed £80 by his Publishers, vanished to the Riviera when he received a cheque for £800. He took his girl friend with him. Computers are not infallible. The matter was settled by the commissioning of a new book and by deducting the £720 from the advance. He was a very good and valuable young author — and he was lucky.

Publisher-Author relations include the covering letter which the author encloses with his manuscript and which can be re-inforced, as I have described, by a copy of the synopsis, the blurb, and also by a brief biographical note of the author. The letter should be brief and businesslike. All that is necessary is:

> "Dear sir,
> I have pleasure in submitting the enclosed manuscript with a view to publication."

That says it all. Personally, I think that it is worth while for a new author to have notepaper printed for him bearing his name, address and telephone number. It is something of a luxury, but it is well worthwhile. This applies even more in the United States where — as in old China — the card and the paper are a part of civilised life, the accepted heralds of the writer announcing his mission or introducing himself.

The new author cannot take too much trouble with this question of approach. If you have sufficient copies it is not necessary to register manuscripts, but many authors do so. At least one knows it has arrived. I favour a firm cover for the manuscript. There are many types of firm cover obtainable at good stationers dealing in this business. Some have the MS pierced and secured. The value arises from the tendency to regard a properly covered MS with a firm backing as a "property". And it is very much less likely to get lost. Such is the rush in many publishers, offices — they are constantly having to meet deadlines — that manuscripts are sometimes lost by both Publishers and authors. The Post Office usually gets the blame — and it is usually innocent.

When correspondence develops, as well it may, the author must be as punctual as the Publisher in replying to correspondence. It was Addison who said: "Despatch is the essence of business." So have all your papers relating to a particular book in one file kept in chronological order. And include the accounts of the business in the file as well. In this way the file will become the executor and trustee of the book. Each move

26

you make as the business develops can reflect its course. By this time you will have begun to realise how your Publisher likes to do business and it is very much in your interest— you will lose nothing and may gain much — to co-operate.

The question is often asked: How long should an author, who has submitted a manuscript to a Publisher with a view to publication, wait before he prods the Publisher with a reminder and a prayer for some indication as to what is happening?

Many Publishers acknowledge the receipt of a manuscript before the book is read and then the author is at least sure that it has arrived and has not been lost. This assurance can be secured by sending a stamped self-addressed envelope. With regard to the even more important subject of the Publisher's reaction, my own experience was, at the beginning of my writing career, that it was a mistake to enquire further for at least a month or six weeks, but if two or three months had elapsed without any word, then a discreet reminder was in order and could not possibly be resented. Publishers are not all the same and authors use their own discretion and tact in dealing with this matter.

If a "property" meets with good sales and publicity when published, the author may well find himself confronted by a variety of offers for "the work" at home and abroad. The basic rule is to read any proposed contract carefully and to understand every word of it. In the writing business you are free to bargain and it will be unusual if you do not do so. Most offers are made at a figure that allows for its increase if the author appears reluctant. Likewise, most demands made by the author allow him to reduce sensibly and still obtain the figure below which he is not prepared to go.

An agent in New York elsewhere may read a book and decide he would like to have an option on it for, say, six months, so that he has the opportunity to sell it as a film or otherwise and to keep out other prospective buyers.

The agreement is in two parts, the Option Agreement itself and "Exhibit A" which is the proposed sale agreement which the Buyer is entitled to have signed by the Seller if he exercises his option within the specified period.

Before approving an option agreement the Author should be informed of the real purpose of the exercise. If, for instance, the objective is to secure the film rights of the book,

27

considerable sums will be involved and the amounts and percentages, as well as the form of the screen credits, are all important.

Option proposals, although often addressed to the author (whom they may suspect is more vulnerable financially than his Publishers) are very much the business of the Author-Publisher relationship. In fact, the franker the Author is with his Publisher and the Publisher with his author, the better it is for both of them. After all, this relationship is covered in all its aspects by the Publisher-Author contract and, although the terms of the agreement may apply only to the book being negotiated, in most cases having written and published one book, both sides hope that they will be able to publish another, after which the Publisher will secure himself by inserting an option clause in the contract. But option or no option, steady friendly relationship is what is being sought by both parties. The Author becomes a regular feature of the Publisher's lists which show his photograph (if he is reasonably photogenic) and carry the blurb of his latest book. It is a business marriage and both parties hope that there will be no divorce.

An alliance of this kind can only endure if both the Publisher and his author are determined it shall and this takes industry, tact and, on occasion, a sense of humour.

CHAPTER 5

Publishers' Contracts

The contract between a Publisher and an author is the legal core of their relationship. It is in writing, must be the result of an offer and an acceptance, and must contain a valuable consideration. Among other matters which the contract will control are: The amount of the advance payable to the author and the time of payment; the percentages or "royalties" paid to the author by the Publisher after the advance has been deducted from the sales; the agreements that cover all subsidiary rights including hardback sales, paperback sales, sales in the country of origin, sales abroad, first and second serial rights, film rights, television and radio rights, and a number of other rights and agreements that cover the whole spectrum of Publisher-author involvement in a book and dictate the share which each is to obtain from any profits from whatever source.

Because the Publisher-author contract is so comprehensive — and so binding — it is up to the author to understand it and all the rights and obligations which it contains. Many authors, when it comes to signing their first contract, consult a lawyer though they do not, as a rule, mention this to the Publisher in case it should interfere with their personal and social relationship. Whether the new author takes this step or not, it is imperative that he understands the contract completely for, once signed, the contract is sacred. Every section must be scrupulously observed in the letter and the spirit. Once signed, it is too late to raise objections to its terms.

Perhaps the easiest way of mastering a Publisher's contract is to quote a typical contract, paragraph by paragraph, and comment on its content and implications.

MEMORANDUM OF AGREEMENT

Made this 4th day of December 1978 BE-
TWEEN The Author (which expression shall
where the context admits include the Author's
executors administrators and assigns) of the
one part and The Publisher of the other part

WHEREBY IT IS MUTUALLY AGREED
AS FOLLOWS

Rights and Ter-
ritory

Length and
delivery date

1. In consideration of the payments hereinafter mentioned the Author hereby grants to the
Publisher the sole and exclusive right to publish (in serial and volume form) for the legal
term of copyright (together with the rights
enumerated in clauses 6, 7 and 8) throughout
the world in any language an original work to
be written by him along the lines already
agreed between the parties hereto at present
provisionally entitled

TITLE OF BOOK

(hereinafter called the said work) which shall
be of not less than 60,000 words in length and
shall be delivered in duplicate to the Publisher
ready for press not later than September 30th
1979

---

*The length of the book is usually kept to within quite a
narrow margin, but it is, of course, impossible for an author to
meet this requirement exactly. The delivery date has to be kept
exactly. The typescript should be in the hands of the Publisher
on the date mentioned.*

Royalties

2. That the publisher shall unless prevented by
circumstances beyond his control publish the
said work under the imprint of The Publisher
(or by mutual agreement under any other

imprint of the Publishing Group) in volume form at a price in the first instance of about £5 net and may subsequently if and when he deems it expedient issue cheaper editions thereof at such prices as he may think advisable and the Publisher shall pay to the Author the following royalty

(a) A royalty of ten per cent (10%) of the published price on all copies sold of the original Home edition up to One thousand five hundred (1,500) copies;

A royalty of twelve and one half per cent (12½%) of the published price on all copies sold of the original Home edition over and above the said One thousand five hundred (1,500) copies and up to Five thousand copies (5,000) copies;

A royalty of fifteen per cent (15%) of the published price on all copies sold of the original Home edition over and above the said Five thousand (5,000) copies

Provided nevertheless that the royalty payable on reprints of two thousand (2,000) copies or less shall be ten per cent

(b) A royalty of ten per cent (10%) of the price obtained on all copies sold overseas or for export.

(c) A royalty to be mutually agreed between the parties hereto on all copies sold of any cheaper editions.

(d) A royalty of ten per cent (10%) of the net cash received for any copies sold as remainders in not less than two years from the date of first publication in pursuance of the Publishers' right in their discretion so to do hereby granted it being provided that such ten per cent (10%) shall be in lieu of the royalties hereinbefore mentioned and that no royalty shall be paid on copies sold at or below cost price.

(e) A royalty of ten per cent (10%) of the net

cash received from the sale of any copies (either bound or in sheets) for the purpose of publication in the United States of America or elsewhere outside the United Kingdom.

(f) On copies sold to the Book Society for sale in the home market ten per cent (10%) of the published price and for export ten per cent (10%) of the Publisher's net receipts.

(g) In the event of the sale to a book club or similar organisation of a licence to reprint the said work the net sum received by the Publishers from the organisation in respect of such licence shall be equally divided between the parties hereto

The royalties set out are customary. Unknown authors may be offered less. Well established authors may be paid more. The ten per cent royalties on net cash received by the Publisher on a wide range of sources of income is common form.

Advance

3. That the Publishers shall pay to the Author the sum of Five Hundred Pounds (£500) in advance and on account of the royalties and all other monies which may become due to him in any way under this agreement and this sum shall be payable as to Two Hundred and Fifty Pounds on the signature of this agreement by both of the parties hereinbefore mentioned and as to the balance within two weeks of the delivery of the completed typescript of the said work.

That in the event of the Author failing to deliver the complete typescript ready for press as provided under Clause 1 hereof he shall unless mutually agreed forthwith repay to the Publishers the whole of that part of the advance already paid to him under this Clause

The advance may be paid on signature of the contract or it may be paid half on signature and half on delivery or it may be paid

only on delivery. This is a clause which the author has to bargain with his Publisher both as to the amount and timing of the payments.

Production etc. at Publishers' discretion

4. The Publisher shall unless prevented by war strikes lock-outs or other circumstances beyond the Publisher's control produce and publish the work at his own risk and expense. The Publisher shall have the entire control of the translation the publication the paper printing binding jacket and embellishments the manner and extent of advertisement the number and distribution of free copies for the Press or otherwise and the price and terms of the first or any subsequent edition shall be in his sole discretion

---

Clause 4 is the main clause covering Publishers' obligations and it is unlikely to be altered.

Copy-right notice

5. That the copyright notice to be printed upon every copy of the said work shall be in the name of Gerald Sparrow (c) with year of first publication

---

The copyright should always belong exclusively to the author and the author must insist that this be so. Most publishers acknowledge this.

---

6. That the Publisher shall control the television rights the first and second serial rights including periodical and newspaper strip-cartoon rights the rights of translation and publication in any foreign language and the rights of publication in English in the United States of America or elsewhere outside the United Kingdom and it is agreed that if the Publishers shall sell such rights eighty per cent (80%) of the net amount received by them shall be paid to the Author and the royalty arrangements mentioned in Clause 2 hereof shall not apply.

Clause 6. There is no dispute or misunderstanding likely to arise out of this clause.

7. That the Publisher shall control the reprint rights (including continental European reprint rights in English) and digest rights the digest-book condensation rights the one-shot (single-issue) periodical and newspaper rights the strip-cartoon (picturisation) book rights and it is agreed that if they shall sell such rights the net amount received by the Publisher from such sale shall be equally divided between the parties hereto

Clause 7. Again there is nothing unfair in this clause. As the Publisher has the responsibility for printing, advertising, sales, distribution etc. it is right that he should have control of these operations. This does not mean that the author may not make suggestions. During the two decades that I was at my busiest I was able on occasion to introduce publishers to valuable contacts which I had come across in the course of my writing career and they welcomed and duly exploited such introductions to our mutual benefit.

8. That the anthology quotation rights and the right to broadcast or make gramophone records of the actual text of the said work and all other rights of mechanical and electrical reproduction (including micro-photography) or any other contrivance shall be controlled jointly by the Author and the Publisher and the proceeds from the sale of them equally divided BUT it is agreed that no fee shall be required for any use by recognised institutions for the blind of the rights mentioned in this Clause.

Clause 8. The joint control provided for in this section is useful for it may well be that in the realm of broadcasting the author's knowledge and experience are as wide as the Publisher's. I was frequently contacted directly by the media and would inform my Publisher accordingly and often, having obtained their consent, they preferred to leave the matter in my hands. The anthology quotation rights, on the other hand, were a matter that they would usually do themselves.

Copy-right and libel warranty

9. That the Author hereby warrants to the Publisher that the said work is not in any way whatever an infringement of any existing copyright and that it contains nothing obscene scandalous indecent blasphemous objectionable libellous or defamatory that all statements contained therein purporting to be facts are true and the Author will indemnify and keep indemnified the Publisher against any loss injury damage (including any legal costs or expenses properly incurred and any compensation costs and disbursements paid by the Publisher on the advice of Counsel to compromise or settle any claim) occasioned to the Publisher in consequence of any breach of this warranty or arising out of any claim alleging that the said work constituted an infringement of copyright or contains libellous or defamatory matter.

This warranty clause, though very widely worded, comes down to the particular facts and circumstances of any claim. During the twenty-two years to date I have never encountered a serious claim against my Publishers. The most serious trap is libel. Most Publishers go to the expense of having a manuscript vetted for libel. But they are not bound to do this. It is not negligent if they rely purely on the author's warranty clause. So the author has to be very careful, adopting the old motto — When in doubt, cut. In a later chapter I enlarge on the dangers of defamation and the best means of avoiding any claim in respect of libel.

10. That if at any time during the continuance of this agreement the copyright in the said work in the reasonable opinion of the Publisher be infringed and the Author after receiving written notice of such infringement

from the Publisher refuses or neglects to take proceedings in respect of the infringement the Publisher shall be entitled to take proceedings in the joint names of the Publisher and the Author upon giving the Author a sufficient and reasonable security to indemnify the Author against any liability for costs and in this event any sum received by way of damages shall belong to the Publisher. If the Author is willing to take proceedings and the Publisher desires to be joined with him as a party thereto and agree to share the costs then if any sum is recovered by way of damages and costs such sum shall be applied in payment of the costs incurred and the balance shall be divided equally between the Author and the Publisher. The provisions of this clause are only intended to apply in the case of the infringement of the copyright in the said work affecting the interest in the same granted to the Publisher under this agreement

---

Clause 10. This is a somewhat curious clause because, as we have pointed out, the copyright belongs exclusively to the Author but the interests of Author and Publisher are intertwined here and the clause is a fair solution to the difficulty.

Author's alterations

11. That the Author shall correct and return the proofs of the said work within fourteen days failing which the Publisher may consider the proofs as passed for press. All charges for alterations other than the correction of printer's errors in excess of ten per cent (10%) of the cost of composition shall be debited to the Author and settled in account.

Author's Alterations. No reasonable Publisher would object if the author needed some extra days to complete proof correction. There are recognised hieroglyphics for this matter, but they are not compulsory. As long as the corrections are perfectly clear they are acceptable — but they will not be clear if they are rushed.

36

Index and Illustrations 12. That the Author shall supply an Index for the said work.

Some authors do their own index. Some prefer to pay an expert. Illustrations are very important to certain types of books and, of course, are the property of the author on loan to the Publisher for reproduction by the printer and returnable to the Author.

Presentation copies 13. That the Author shall be entitled to receive on publication six presentation copies of the first edition of the said work and to purchase further copies for personal use (but not for resale) at two-thirds of the published price.

Clause 13. This clause is self-explanatory and customary.

14. That the Author shall not write or publish or be concerned directly or indirectly in writing or publishing any other book on the same subject or of any such a kind or published at such a price as may reasonably be considered by the Publisher as liable to affect injuriously the sale of the said work while the Publisher still has the said work in print.

Clause 14. There is no objection to this Clause.

15. That if at any time when a new edition may be contemplated the Author is not available after reasonable efforts have been made to establish contact with him or if the Author does not undertake revision the Publisher shall have the right to amend or expand the book as he thinks fit at his expense.

Clause 15. The author would do well to be available if a new edition is contemplated. The Publisher should always have his current address and telephone number whether he is at home or abroad.

16. That if at any time the Publisher allows the said work to go out of print or off the market in all editions and within nine months after receiving written notice from the Author so to do he has not reprinted and placed on the market a new edition then all rights of printing publishing and selling the said work as granted under this agreement shall forthwith at the expiration of the said period of nine months revert to the Author (but not those deriving from the option in Clause 19 hereof) without prejudice to any existing contracts entered into by the Publisher prior to the date of such reversion and relating to subsidiary rights vested in them here.

Out of print. This clause seems to arise out of the logic of an "out of print" situation.

17. That on copies given away to the Author or for the purpose of aiding the sale or for review or on copies accidentally destroyed the Publisher shall be free of any liability to pay royalty.

Clause 17. This clause applies substantially to review copies which may concern from fifty to a hundred copies. No royalty is due to the author because these copies are given to promote sales, to interest the critics, and in general in the interests of the Author and Publisher.

18. That the Publisher shall make up the first two accounts of the said work as at the 30th day of June and the 31st day of December following the date of first publication of the said work and subsequently annually as at the 31st day of December and the said accounts shall be delivered on or before the following 1st day of October and the 1st day of April and any amount found due shall be settled by cash within one month after those dates respectively provided however that no state-

ment need be submitted to the Author unless specifically demanded nor settlement made in respect of any period in which the sum shown to be due is less than one pound (£1) in which case the amount will be carried forward to the next accounting date.

Clause 18. It is always puzzling to authors why Publisher's accounts made up to the end of June and December should not be delivered until October and April and paid a month after that. Building Societies do much better than this and Banks manage prompt payment, too. The explanation is that these great institutions calculate accounts — and interest — on a day to day basis whereas, Publishers, immersed in the day to day business of their own profession, have traditionally made their accounts bi-annually in arrears. It has to be accepted. Publishers, however, can be more humane than the large financial organisations and, after fifteen years, I still remember with gratitude the Publisher who telegraphed me £200 in Beirut where I had to be admitted to hospital with an ulcer.

Option
19. That the Author shall give the Publisher the first refusal of the same rights to commission (including the first opportunity to read and consider for publication) the Author's next two works of a similar nature which he shall write after the work the subject of this agreement on terms and conditions to be mutually agreed which shall be fair and reasonable.

Clause 19. The option clause often refers to one work not two, but if the relationship has developed, as it should, into a stable one of mutual confidence these option clauses are mutually advantageous.

Right of Assignment
20. That the expression "the Publisher" as used throughout this agreement shall be deemed to include the person or persons or Company for the time being carrying on the business or of any other imprint of the Group as aforesaid whether under its present or any

future style and the benefit of this agreement shall be transmissible accordingly.

Clause 20. This right of assignment is usually included in all Publisher's contracts.

21. That the said work is the option called for under Clause 19 of the contract dated between the parties hereto.

Clause 21. This clause merely identifies an "exercised" option.

Publisher-Author contracts are usually in duplicate, the Author retaining the copy signed by the Publisher and the Publisher keeping the copy signed by the author. Both copies are witnessed.

Authors may well be surprised— though they should not be — at the punctilious way in which the majority of Publishers conduct business. On occasion, authors have been depicted as less business-like. I do not think this is any longer fair if it ever was. In any case, the Publisher writes the contract in the first instance (though its terms are subject to mutual agreement) and this arrangement should protect both parties.

This being the core of the contract business the wise author will approach the matter with polite vigilance (as the Publisher does), remembering that friendship and good relations — in the long run — are often more valuable and rewarding than minor victories on comparatively unimportant points.

CHAPTER 6

Publisher-Author Co-operation

When the author has a completed, corrected manuscript, as we have pointed out, he should choose his publisher with the utmost care. Publishers come in all sizes and some of them have comprehensive lists while others specialise. The author, with the aid of the *Writers' and Artists' Yearbook*, and by checking the type of current books which the publisher is supplying to the libraries and to the book shops, can fit his manuscript into the right haven. Time spent on this operation is well worth while. It is most frustrating to submit a manuscript to a publisher only to find that your kind of book is not included in his particular list. Patient checking can avoid this unnecessary hazard.

When the author has chosen the right publisher and the publisher has shown an interest in the manuscript most of the author's work, but not all, is completed, whereas the publisher is just starting the long skilled business which will result in the raw manuscript becoming a finished product as a book to be launched into the market.

The publisher has shown his interest either by a letter, or by telephoning the author, suggesting a meeting and this is the start of negotiations which will result either in the book being published or in the parties being unable to arrive at an agreement. Very often the publisher may suggest alterations or additions to the text of the manuscript. During the twenty years that I have been in the writing business I have almost invariably found these suggestions practical and helpful, improving the work and not in any way detracting from the original version. If this happens I think the author does well in his own interest to go along with the publisher until the manuscript is regarded as publishable by both.

As soon as the publisher is happy with the finalised manuscript the question of a contract arises. I have already dealt with the substance of a typical publisher-author contract. Until this stage is reached the author has no guarantee that he will achieve a contract. He should certainly not take for granted that the extra work which he has done at the suggestion of his publisher gives him any kind of right, legal or moral, that contracts will be exchanged. However, assuming that at this stage the publisher has decided to publish, then he will make an offer to the author both as to the advance and as to the royalty percentages. The author has then three alternatives, to accept without reservation, to negotiate, or to go elsewhere. It is general experience that negotiation leading to both publisher and author agreeing that the deal is fair, is probably the best of these alternatives.

This is the course of events as far as the author is concerned but before the publisher makes an offer the latter has a great deal of work to do, the exact nature of which depends to a large extent on the size of the publishing House. In the case of a small publisher it may be a matter of one man making the decision after he has submitted the manuscript to a "reader" who will provide him with criticism of the work in all its aspects— its literary merit, its interest to the general public or to the specialised public to whom it is directed, its viability and cohesion as a story and, in general, a commentary on its merits and deficiencies.

The publisher then has to make up his mind whether to publish or not but before he does this he will of course go into the financial side of the matter. In particular he will attempt to gauge the potential sales at home and abroad, the possibility of selling serial rights, whether the book will translate easily into other main foreign languages, the price which he should charge for it, that is to say the publisher's price to the bookseller. Each of these questions contains imponderables but the experienced publisher, as well as taking into account each of the calculations I have mentioned, will rely on his own experience and flair. Publishers develop a "nose" for publishable and profitable books just as the wine taster does for good wine and certainly in small publishing houses it is this final factor that counts. Experienced publishers will tell you that in seven cases out of ten their judgment is right. Only rarely do they turn down a book which later is a success altough, of course, these cases do happen and some of the most profitable books have been declined by several publishers. In my observation these rare errors of judgment usually occur when the public taste is changing but the change has not yet revealed itself such as, for instance, the see-saw between complicated, sophisticated novels based on sexual eccentricity and the simple love story.

In the bigger publishing Houses the assessment of a manuscript is done in far greater depth. The editing of the manuscript will be very thorough and the readers' reports will be studied from all angles. Every avenue of potential profit will be explored including first and second serial rights, television and radio rights, possible exploitation as a stage play or musical, potential sales in the United States and Canada, sales in Europe, African and Middle and Far Eastern sales, sales in the Spanish speaking world, that is, in South America with the exception of Brazil. In addition the format of the book will be very carefully studied. Is it a natural hard-back which may sell as a paperback later? Or is its length and make-up more suited to production as a paperback?

In the big publishing House the costing entailed in the publication of a particular book will contain detailed assessments of every possible expense including, of course, printing, marketing and advertising.

The author should realise that the publisher has gone through a fairly long and complicated process of assessment before he makes his offer for the book and in the case of a reputable publisher — and most publishers are reputable — the offer made will be a fair reflection of what the author should be entitled to. However, publishers are only human and, unless they are extremely enthusiastic about a book their initial offer will tend to be conservative. They must always have two targets in mind, the first to avoid a loss on the operation and the second to make a profit. Incidentally, these two objectives are identical with that of the bookmaker in the racing world but the bookmaker has an additional security inasmuch as he can "lay off the odds".

There are two matters that the author is responsible for at a later stage. The first is the correction of the proofs of the book. These will usually consist of galley-proofs but there are a number of modern methods of reproducing the manuscript for correction which entail the same kind of work for the author. The correction of the proofs is an author's obligation and will be provided for in a clause of his contract. There is a classified and agreed number of signs which should be used in the correction of proofs and are often used by publishers and printers but most authors find these signs too technical and prefer to correct the proofs without resorting to them. Provided the author's corrections are immediately clear to the publisher and to the printer this is quite satisfactory because clarity is the whole point of the exercise, however it may be achieved, but nothing is more infuriating to a printer working to a deadline than to have to ask what a particular correction means. Time is wasted, machinery may have to be halted and the correction of a correction has been known to obscure the intended reading even more. So proof reading is a serious obligation which the author owes to his publisher and his publisher's printer. It is unprofessional to fall down on proof correction. The publisher will often indicate the date by which he would like to have the corrected proof returned and this date, too, should be strictly kept. Personally I think it worthwhile that in all dealings with a publisher dates agreed should be kept meticulously so that the publisher actually receives what he is expecting on the agreed date rather than some days later due to postal delays.

The next obligation of the author is to provide any Index that may be required. The author has the choice of either compiling the Index himself or of paying someone to undertake this somewhat laborious work. Whichever method he chooses, the Index must contain all the chief characters in the book and the subjects it deals with. It will usually be necessary to include place names and, in fact, a good Index should be a key that will enable the reader to be guided to every substantial aspect of the book. Authors who do their own Indexing have different methods of achieving this. My own method is first to check the book page by page and extract what should be in the Index, noting the page number of each item, then to place the references in alphabetical order and to refine this process to the third letter of the word. After this, to make the entries on a large sheet of paper about a yard square and then to have the finished product typed on ordinary typing paper from which the printer can make his print without difficulty. In the care and correctness which the author achieves in Indexing, as in other matters, his professionalism will reveal itself and the smooth working of publisher-author-printer relations will be enhanced.

There are additional matters which the publisher has the right and obligation to do himself according to the terms of the contract and according to custom but it is possible that when a publisher is dealing with an experienced author he may accept suggestions from the author which are as helpful to him as the suggestions which he makes to the author regarding the manuscript. If I may give a personal example, the late Sir William Collins, when he published my book, *The Green Garuda*, gladly accepted a cover design which was brilliantly executed by Eric Rogers and which showed the Phoenix-like figure of Siamese mythology in a way that completely identified the book and was most effective and striking from a sales point of view. This was exceptional, for most publishers have cover artists who perhaps have worked for them for years and have achieved great skill in this specialised form of art. The cover of the book is, of course, its window to the world and for this reason is important and should be significant.

Advertising is solely the province of the publisher who, as he bears all the expense, will rightly regard this as an area in which his expertise can greatly help the sale of the book. However, if the author is known to television and radio in the Capital and in the Provinces and is willing to appear in programmes on which the book is discussed, no publisher is going to refuse this bonus. The audience for a well established national television programme runs into many millions and this operation provides the author with a unique opportunity of assisting the sales of his book and incidentally of making himself known in a personal way to a very wide public. There are a number of ways in which it is suggested authors in this situation can make an effective appearance on television as well as on radio but I think that the basic rule is to be completely natural. Someone who is obviously sincere is certainly more attractive than someone who is striving for effect. Authors usually have such a good opinion of themselves that they will not be unduly nervous but audiences tend to react against brashness or any inclination to lecture them. If some humour can be introduced into the subject being discussed this, too, will help because the world does not laugh enough and most viewers warm to a programme which tends to amuse as well as to instruct them.

If the author is fortunate enough to have an attractive

house or flat he may like to have a party for the Press on publication day, but publishers often do this themselves or the publisher and author may join in the enterprise. The people invited, of course, tend to be the Press and the critics but it does no harm if a contentious politician or a beautiful and talented actress graces the scene. There is a school of thought that such receptions get nowhere at all but personally I reserve judgment on this. The benefits are usually not tangible and immediately discernable, but this does not mean that they do not exist.

The publisher is always the key figure in the entire operation of book production. Of course, he cannot produce a book until some author has written a suitable manuscript for his list but when that is done the whole matter with all its off-shoots depends on him. He is the man who puts up the money and he has a right to control the steps that should be taken and how problems that may arise should be solved. Although the author stands or falls by the quality of his writing and by the sales and critical reaction to his book, the publisher is just as deeply concerned with success. While a fine book will enhance the reputation of the publisher with other publishers, with the book trade, and with the general public, a poor book which does not sell will do him harm, and his aim is constantly to improve the image of his business so that he extends his operations and acquires a larger and more imposing List. Eventually he hopes to reach a stage where the name of his firm is a household word synonomous, in the public estimation, with good publishing. There are books which few publishers will refuse, for instance the intimate revelations of a President or Prime Minister; there are books of such outstanding literary merit that the publisher will take on the risk of publishing them although he may not be sure of a profit at the end of the road; and there are border line books which are good, but are they good enough? The publisher is constantly having to make difficult decisions.

Publishers are not in the happy position of bankers who are able to lend money against property or shares. The publisher has to invest money without security except that which is represented by a manuscript which may be an asset or may be a liability. The author, on the other hand, unless he is commissioned to write the book, has to devote a year or six months of his time and skill to the research and writing of the book

46

without the assurance that he will be able to sell it at the end of the road. Both publishers and authors, then, are in a risk business and it is up to them to help each other as much as is possible by a smooth and helpful co-operation. Only the printer gets paid automatically for the work he does and as we have pointed out, even the printer may be subjected to claims for damages by libel should such claims ever arise.

There are easier and more certain ways of making money than publishing or authorship. It must be the elements of excitement and achievement involved in their work that sustain the publisher and the author and make them happy to overcome all the hardships in the hope of achieving gratifying success. There is no more exciting reward to both parties than when a book "runs away". The printer cannot produce fast enough. The book shops are insatiable in their demands and the enquiries for serial rights start to come in. It is not an experience that publishers, however successful, enjoy very often, but when it comes then the tribulations are forgotten for a time and author and publisher realise, perhaps with incredulity, that they have launched what may honestly be described as a best seller.

CHAPTER 7

The Variety of Choice

Apart from *belle-lettres* which, if they still exist, are described as serious and polite literary studies, presumably written for the connoisseur, biography and important autobiography are regarded as the top of the writing tree. They deserve that prestigious place because they entail deeper research, more intimate contact, and great skill.

The biographer finds that in order to portray his subject, to an extent, he has to become his subject. Certainly he has to penetrate completely the outer layer of social covering that most people wear to protect themselves from the poisoned arrows of life and the envious little people who hurl them. The biographer has to be compassionate and ruthless, honest and humorous, skilled and possessing that quality of ease and conviction that conceals the exercise of a difficult craft and the endless research that has gone before.

In a sense the biographer has a man's life in his hands. The subject is on trial and at the end of the book a verdict must be chosen: Guilty or Not Guilty, or that logical and useful Scottish verdict of Not Proven. The conclusion of guilt will only be evoked when the subject is a wicked person by any human standards. History has provided and still provides such characters.

Above all the biographer must have integrity like the painter. He can never say: "That is what this man was." But he must always be able to say: "That is this man as I see him, portrayed without malice and without fear."

Desmond MacCarthy said: "The biographer is an artist on oath." While Rebecca West put it splendidly in these words: "The art of biography, we say— but at once we go on to ask, is biography an art? The artist's imagination at its most intense fires out what is perishable, in fact he builds what is durable; but the biographer must accept the perishable, build with it, imbed it in the very fabric of his work. Much will perish, little will live. And thus we come to the conclusion that the biographer is a craftsman not an artist, and his work is not a work of art but something betwixt and between."

If one has a comment to make on this could it be that biography requires the skills of both the artist and the craftsman and that the good biographer will certainly be both crafty and artistic. But, given good writing, is not honesty all?

During the last century biographies have abandoned adulation for denigration, but the best biographies are still those in which the scale is held evenly. We do not expect our heroes to be angels any more. Yet in Victorian times the heroic uncritical biography was published and apparently read without any explosive reaction. I have in front of me *The Life of Arthur, Duke of Wellington* by G.R. Gleig M.A., published by Longman Green in 1890. It is the most beautiful book. The paper is still dazzlingly white. The print is impeccable. The pages are tipped with gold. The cover is in leather and the inscriptions are all in gold. It is a joy to handle. It is not a joy to read. It is a book of monumental dullness. It achieves the almost impossible task of making a swashbuckling, clever Anglo-Irish aristocrat into an automaton who fought a number of memorable battles which he usually won. Even at the end of the book, when all the wars are over and he is Prime Minister no longer, but living at Walmer Castle, it is his habit of dress we are allowed to recall in detail:

> His morning dress, as a civilian, was scrupulously neat and clean, but varied very little, and that only with the change of seasons. In summer he might be recognised, on foot or on horseback, by his low-crowned narrow-brimmed hat, his white cravat fastened with a silver buckle behind; his blue frock, white waistcoat and white trowsers. In winter there were the same hat, neckcloth and frock, with a waistcoat blue, sometimes red, and blue trousers. He never wore a great coat, but in severe weather threw a short cloak or cape over his shoulders, made of blue cloth, with a white lining. His evening attire, except when he was in mourning, consisted of a blue coat, with metal buttons, a white cravat and waistcoat, black breeches, and silk stockings,

or tight black pantaloons. On these occasions he wore the order of the Garter under the left knee, with the Golden Fleece suspended round his neck, the blue or other ribbon, and a star. When at Walmer, he often dressed for dinner in the uniform of the Cinque Ports, viz. a blue coat with a scarlet collar and cuffs, and blue trowsers with a red stripe down the outer seam.

This is perhaps the most intimate glimpse of Arthur Wellesley we are allowed to see. His military mistakes are carefully explained away, his great success described with what amounts to reverence. Never for a moment are we allowed to as much as peep at a mistress, or to hear the Duke in full roar when his Irish blood was boiling, and he was berating someone who had failed in his duty. And we are not even permitted to hear the Duke exercising that blend of forthrightness and humour that appealed to Queen Victoria when she believed herself to be confronted with a "situation".

We would expect an old soldier to be neat and tidy and it does not surprise us that his boots were polished or his linen clean. This was decorous biography at its most unrevealing.

Rebecca West would never admit it, but perhaps it takes a cad to write a good stinging biography. Lytton Strachey stirred up his complacent public by exposing the failings, foibles, indiscretions and hypocrisy of some revered personalities but his spite spoilt the attacks. He was so vulnerable himself. Frank Harris's biography of his friend and benefactor, Bernard Shaw, comes near to betraying him. Two of the best biographies of recent times seemed to me to be the superb biography of Sir Edward Marshall Hall. "Marshall" leaps right out of the pages — just as he was; and Lord Birkenhead's more monumental biography of the late Lord Halifax which, though it does not seek to unmask, perhaps because its subject was that forgotten species, the "English gentleman", does evoke — sometimes with painful force and clarity — the "Chamberlain era" before and during the early stages of the last world war.

The younger writers — now, alas, becoming middle-aged — such as Colin Wilson and David Irving, are much to be admired for their research. Both write well but what comes through strongly is their mastery of their subject. If in the years ahead they turn to biography we will be able to enjoy some fine books by masters of the writing profession.

Autobiography, perhaps easier than biography because by definition it does not pretend to be impartial, is a weakness with authors. Most of their books, one way or another, are in parts autobiographical. A young Communist cannot write a book on the British establishment without letting his views come through, nor for that matter can a young Fascist. And if they write a novel the heroine will not be the Squire's daughter but some sexually adult nymph just graduated from the London School of Economics.

Very few young men write autobiographies but if they have a flair for reality this will compensate for the lack of experience, for ideally a man should write his autobiography while he is still close to the world which was his own. Autobiography suffers if it is too mellow. Old men tend to forgive — and to forget.

Eccentrics sometimes write excellent autobiographies. J.S. Mills said: "That so few now dare to be eccentric marks the chief danger of our times." The irregular fellow usually has something different to say. The regular fellow, "the great guy" of contemporary American mythology, whether he has excelled in politics or sport, often makes deadly reading.

So should you venture into autobiography? If you do, you will have to be exceptionally talented. Your Publisher will write you a polite little note explaining how difficult it is to sell biography of any kind unless it has as its subject a personality who is already a household word to the public, or even better, a world figure whose literary portrait may procure sales world wide.

These warnings of vicissitudes are not good cheer for the new author so let us explore the other fields he may find easier.

1. *The Novel*. In theory everyone can write a potentially saleable novel. The novel covers all life. All "classes", all colours, all politics, all faiths, all human relations, marriage, divorce and cohabitation. It is all grist to the novel's mill. This is the sphere of the writing profession that has no boundaries.

2. *Crime*. This is a rich field for those who have the

specialised knowledge. Crime can be exploited by the author in diverse ways. Books have been written on crime in general — the psychology of crime — crime and society. Teenage crime, professional and amateur crime. Women criminals. Great forgers, great traitors, great robbers.

Crime and Punishment, prisons, the prison system, parole. Murderers, murder for money, murder for love, revenge murder and, perhaps most despicable of all, murders politically motivated. The field is endless and because the criminal is a nonconformist he constantly fascinates and infuriates a society whose lives are based on respect for the law. The death penalty alone needs a book. So few have written about it impartially and with knowledge. It is a subject that seems to provoke irrational discussion on both sides. The police, the crime detectors and preventers, are vital sources from the author's point of view, and so is Scotland Yard and forensic science on which so much modern detection now rests.

So here is a wide and varied field for the new author. It includes crime today in Britain, the United States, Europe and elsewhere. It can cover historical crime when the author's gift of recreating an atmosphere will be essential. Crime may or may not pay those who practise it, but certainly the author, who is prepared to write on it with knowledge and research and eventually become recognised as an authority, can turn crime into royalties and fill that section on his Publisher's list that is devoted to crime and criminals.

3. *Travel and Tourism*. Again, a growing market for those who have the knowledge.

4. *Adventure*. Read Richard Pape's *Boldness be my Friend*. This is the stuff of which adventure is made.

5. *Sport*. There is a constant demand for books on sport.

6. *Specialised Books*. Gardening, cooking, do-it-yourself.

7. *Space Fiction*. But, be careful. It is advancing all the time and you should have a new — and startling — approach.

8. *The Countryside*. Farming, rural pursuits, out-of-the-way places and people. Have a look at Priestley to

see how it is done.

9. *Faction*. Books based on reality but given the author's treatment, and the benefit of his imagination.

10. *Factual Books*. These include autobiography and biography.

11. It is not uncommon for a great institution or a well-known firm, perhaps celebrating their centenary, to commission an author to write a full book, or a booklet, telling their story, perhaps from small beginnings through struggles to success and wide public service. They do not always choose an established author. A new author, who is prepared to delve into the history of the subject and who then approaches the Directors with a proposal which reveals intimate knowledge and a wide and balanced view of their enterprise, has a chance of being commissioned to write such a book — and once an author has done one such book with success, another may follow and a valuable source of income may be established.

There are other fields and there are streams off the main river and these, too, are worth exploring.

The best asset a new author can have is determination. Always finish a book. Never give up. Never surrender. If one publisher does not like your work, another may — and he may be right. Some first-rate books, which have established their authors, have survived half-a-dozen refusals.

CHAPTER 8

Films, Radio and Television

The opportunities for writers presented by the stage play or "musical", television and broadcasting, are immense but the obstacles to entering any one of these outlets are considerable. Take, as an example, the television play and the sale of film rights.

The sale of film rights is the most likely field that a new author, if he has had a successful book published, is likely to enter. Often the interest will be shown by the film company concerned. Their talent spotters read new books that are well reviewed and deal with a subject that the company regard as fashionable and saleable as a film to the public.

The author may, in consultation with his Publisher, approach a film company with a synopsis and, on reading this, a dialogue and a course of negotiation may develop which leads at first to an option, and secondly a sale of film rights. The names, addresses and telephone numbers of the main film companies are given in the invaluable *Writers' and Artists' Year Book*. The company will certainly have its own form of contract which will fully protect their interests and it is up to the author to protect himself. However, as the Publisher of the book has a share in the sale, he, too, will be concerned and, as most publishers have regular lawyers acting for them — even if only in an advisory capacity, it may well be that the author himself does not have to go to the expense of employing lawyers. American film companies, for the right book, usually pay the best price. On the other hand, they are renowned for formidable bargaining and the price first offered may be only a fraction of the ultimate price which they have in mind and beyond which they are not prepared to go. Many writers, as this becomes a process of mind reading, believe that for the sale of film rights it is well worth employing an agent who may increase the initial offer by far more than his percentage fee which, for many years, was 10% but has of late tended to be 12½% or 15%.

Television, of course, is divided into— in this country— the BBC and Commercial Television. The latter usually are more generous, the BBC more prestigious. Radio plays are in a class by themselves. In neither case does one have to accept the first offer.

And now the crucial question arises: How does the new author learn how to write a stage play, a film script, a television play or a radio play? He can, of course, enrol with one of the numerous correspondence courses that are offered. But, from my personal experience, I have found that there is only one sure way of learning this business. It costs nothing but requires close attention and intelligence. Borrow from a writer one of his scripts in the area you wish to exploit and read every word of it, making notes of the technique and remembering it all. Writers are as a rule willing to help a new writer in this way. The script will not be the one he is at present concerned with. It will be a past success. But it will all be there. Let us take an illustration from a script. The scene is set in the Shan States.

SOMCHA bows and smiles and leads them down into the Palace cellars. In this dungeon a few feet apart are a dozen bamboo cages in which a man cannot stand upright but is caged like a monkey. All the cages contain a man and three contain two men who can hardly move. At the end of the line of cages is one padded cell — empty.

PRINCESS
These are the disobedient ones.
Their offences vary. Petty disobedience
of my orders, secreting their crops, trying
to sell privately, unruly and disloyal
behaviour.

(In three of the cages the men are in the grip of hallucinations and are grovelling in an agony of nightmare and torment. The remainder are sullen and morose.)

PRINCESS
The lively ones are just locked up. For
the first time in their lives they are not
receiving opium. They are being broken.
The silent ones are broken. They will be
released after they have been beaten,
and they will never disobey again. Crude
but true.

JONATHAN
But they must hate you ....

PRINCESS
Oh no. They will do anything, anything
to get the drug back again. (She speaks in
Shan to SOMCHA) Look, I will show
you.

They stop at the cage of a silent prisoner, SOMCHA takes a
brown pill from his pocket and holds it out to the man who
springs to seize it .... But SOMCHA draws it back and speaks
to the man in his own language giving a peremptory order ...
    The man holds out his left hand supported at the elbow by
his right and, kneeling, puts his upstretched hand through the
bars to the Princess. The Princess stubs out her lighted
cheroot in the palm of the man's hand. He winces but does not
cry out.

PRINCESS
Give him his reward.

SOMCHA hands the man the pill who swallows it smiling. He
is transformed by the drug and quickly his stature returns. He
is a man again.

PRINCESS
Now JONATHAN you know. They will
never revolt. How can they? No opium,
no life. And opium depends on me. I
cage them and they become animals.
They *are* animals....

56

JONATHAN
It's vile. It's monstrous.

PRINCESS
Oh come now. You keep your battery hens in cages all their lives to lay you eggs. They never know freedom. They are caged for life. They cannot even move freely. These men are here for a few days, are taught their lesson, and released ...

JONATHAN
But these are men, not animals ...

PRINCESS
They *are* animals. If they had power and money and "rights" there would be chaos. They would rape and murder and drink themselves to death — alcohol and opium, the world's quickest killers. As it is they live in the sunlight! Working not too hard, loving when they want, sleeping at night with their golden dreams... They are happier this way ... Freedom is a word, JONATHAN. I choose my men carefully. SOMCHA is not nice to look at, but he has two great virtues ...

JONATHAN
And they are?

PRINCESS
He inspires terror, and he would die for me ...

Let us suppose that the film rights of your book have been sold to a film company. They can then hire you or another author to write the script of the film or they can contract their own writer and make an arrangement with you to act in an advisory capacity because they believe that you may know the subject and perhaps the venue of the book better than anyone else and will be able to ensure that the script is authentic. There are several different arrangements that may be made.

If you are commissioned to write the script then you must learn quickly the technicalities of the craft and this, as I have pointed out, you can best do from a real script.

You will see that there are certain distinctions you must have clearly in your mind as a script-writer. The film may open with a scene, possibly and preferably with action shown through the "credits". This scene — unspoken — may set the whole atmosphere and climate for your story. It is very important. You are now writing for the camera. Remember that you are always writing for the camera and usually for the actors. Your script must be explicit. It must tell the Director, the camera crew and the actors exactly what is going on.

When you have finished one scene you indicate this by some phrase such as "We track back to". When you come to dialogue you must indicate it clearly. "Wardlaw is speaking to his clerk, Harold Tomkins." When there is a break in the dialogue it must be distinct. Dialogue lines are usually short. Directions and descriptive writing full length across the page. Once you have set the scene and the characters it may not be necessary to indicate the changes so explicitly. The difference between dialogue and description will be manifest from the type setting of the page.

Dialogue, as always, is better kept crisp and clear. You, the script writer, must make every movement, every word and every action crystal clear to the cast who will have to act the script. The fewer writer directions the better but above all there must never be a doubt as to what is happening, where it is happening, to whom it is happening and who is speaking. Directions may be small — "Jane whispers to her sister" — or more detailed — "Arthur is about to read on, but what he sees frightens him and he hesitates..."

When the characters are engaged in action without dialogue the script-writer must take over. Directions and description carry on until dialogue starts again. When you have absorbed one good film script you will be ready to attempt to write a script yourself. Do not get bogged down in technicalities. Your first task is to get and keep the story strong, moving, convincing. If you do not feel moved by what is going on, no-one else will be. In dialogue, the name of the speaker is usually printed in block capitals over each piece of dialogue to avoid any possible confusion. In time you will find that you can write a script almost as easily as you can write a novel. As soon as you remember effortlessly that your script has to be acted and spoken then you will have accomplished one of the big leaps in the writing business. It will give you great satisfaction. You will have given an entirely new dimension to your original book. You will have made it come alive in a different and dramatic medium. When I wrote my first film script and sold my first film rights I realised I had entered a new world. It was wonderful.

Because potentially large money is involved in all film negotiations and business, the Publisher and author of the book on which the film is based must take great care. Because most film companies have their favourite screen writers, and this applies even more strongly to the BBC which is a fraternity of talent, there may well be an attempt to buy the script as a basis for their own script. This may suit the film company but not the author because, at the end of the road, his script is submerged and the screen credits will go to the writers of the company. All the author will get is an "acknowledgment", often in fairly small print, that the story is "based on" the book by the author. It suggests he writes the kind of books that may make good films, but it advances his career as a script writer not at all. Business is not a tea-party and the jockeying for position would often incur an enquiry by the stewards if they existed. *Caveat vendor* is as important as *caveat emptor* in this world of tough negotiation.

Before embarking on the wide and sometimes rough seas of the film world, the new author would be well advised to explore the possibilities of a radio play. The techniques are much the same as a film, but there are differences. In a radio play, as opposed to a television play, everything depends on the spoken word. The characters are not seen, the action is not seen, the location is not seen. Everything depends on dialogue and it is through dialogue that the action, the scene, the players' characters and every nuance has to be conveyed, as well as the appearance of the actor and the movement of the story. It is not easy but it is much easier than a film and makes a good nursery. As the cast are all together at a microphone the cost of production is quite small, indeed, only a fraction of film cost.

May I relate my own experience, not because it is better than anyone else's, but because it is authentic. It happened to me so it can happen to you.

A congenial producer at the BBC asked me if I could write a radio play. I had never even considered the matter but I had confidence and said, "Yes." I immediately borrowed two scripts from a friendly writer, read them carefully — twice — and knew I could do the work.

I wrote six radio plays before getting involved in films. It was a most helpful experience.

I quote the opening directions of a play I wrote for television founded on the story of Thomas Goudie, a Scottish son of the manse, employed by the Bank of Liverpool as a Ledger Clerk, who stole £150,000 from the account of Mr Hudson (a soap manufacturer), lost it betting on racehorses, and was blackmailed by three thugs known as the Light, the Shadow of the Light and the Shadow of the Shadow of the Light.

THE BANK CLERK

Proposed sets

1. The Bank of Liverpool, in the centre of the City of Liverpool, in 1900. This shows in particular the row of Ledger Clerks, each with his own "cubicle", each responsible, and taking a great pride in his Ledger, more especially Goudie's Ledger A to H. Also the Cashiers' counter; and the seat, behind the Ledger Clerks, of Mr Pinto, the Chief Clerk. The door of the office of the Manager, Mr Appleton, is to the right. His office is spacious, traditional, comfortable.

Note. I have a sketch of the Ledger Clerk's desk including his seat, his shelf for resting the Ledger, and the general posture and position of Thomas at work.

2. A racecourse. Preferably in the North of England — Aintree, or even at Newmarket. This set really only shows the Bookmakers ring, or a section of it. The racing itself is suggested rather than portrayed.

3. "SAM'S KITCHEN" A little Liverpool restaurant frequented by Thomas and by George and Fay.

4. A bedroom at Thomas's pound-a-week lodgings in Paradise Street, Liverpool.

ACT 1.   THE OFFICE OF THE MANAGER OF THE BANK OF LIVERPOOL IN 1901. A ROOM OF FORMIDABLE RESPECTABILITY WITH ONE VAST DESK, LEATHER CHAIRS, A SIDEBOARD FOR SHERRY AND CAKE, AND PORTRAITS OF THE FOUNDER ON THE WALLS.

MR APPLETON, THE MANAGER, SEATED, IS SPEAKING TO THE CHIEF CLERK, MR PINTO, WHO STANDS DEFERENTIALLY AT HIS SIDE. MR APPLETON IS TURNING OVER A SHEAF OF PAPERS.

APPLETON.
Are they good for another five thousand, Mr Pinto?

PINTO.
I think so, Sir, but I feel that should be the limit.

APPLETON (endorsing a file) Very well. Five thousand. No more. Any other business?

PINTO. There is a new Ledger Clerk, Sir. Thomas Goudie. I have his letters here. (He hands them to Appleton)

APPLETON. Twenty-nine, eh? Father a parson. Good. Intelligent, these people say, and absolutely honest. Looks all right. What do you think?

PINTO. I suggest you see him, Sir. He's asking two hundred a year. Ridiculous, of course. But, at a price, he seems the right type.

APPLETON. Let's have a look at him.

PINTO. (Going to the door, opening it and beckoning to Thomas who is waiting outside) Come in now.

THOMAS GOUDIE, INTELLIGENT, GOOD LOOK-
ING IN A WEAK WAY, SOBERLY DRESSED,
ENTERS AND STANDS BEFORE MR APPLETON'S
DESK.

MR APPLETON. So you wish to join us? What
makes you think we might accept your services?

GOUDIE. I heard you needed an experienced
Ledger Clerk, Sir. I am experienced — and willing to work hard.

MR APPLETON. Prepared to work hard, eh?
You'll *have* to work hard if we take you on.
What's this I hear about two hundred a year?
Four pounds a week! You're joking.

GOUDIE. No, sir. I thought I was worth that.
It's a responsible position. I would have to record
correctly a great number of large transactions...

MR APPLETON. You young men are all alike.
Out for the last penny! No consideration at all.
We pay our Ledger Clerks three pounds a week,
rising by annual instalments of ten shillings a
week. They say we're over-generous, but there
you are. Take it or leave it...

GOUDIE. I accept, Sir.

Then towards the end of the play the author makes use of
an extract from the Liverpool press describing the climax of
the case:

Pinto, the Manager's Assistant, is reading.

PINTO. (Reading) "The sensational fraud on the
Bank of Liverpool which has been the talk of
business and banking circles for months past
(Appleton groans) ended today in the Assize
Court when, before Lord Mersey (Mr Justice
Bigham) Thomas Goudie, described as a Ledger
Clerk of the Bank of Liverpool, pleaded guilty to

embezzling over £160,000 of the funds of the Bank and to seven other charges of larceny and forgery. Mr F.E. Smith, speaking in mitigation of sentence, said that perhaps never before, in the annals of crime, had a man enjoyed so little of the fruits of his fraud. Goudie had been in the hands first of a couple of plausible tricksters, and then of a terrifying race-course gang. He had helped the Bank to recover three quarters of the stolen money.

"Lord Mersey sentenced Goudie to seven years penal servitude, and said it was a protracted, deliberate fraud and no lesser sentence was possible."

It is evident that this play entailed considerable research.

The whole fraud was only made possible by the fact that each Ledger Clerk had absolute control over the customers' accounts between certain letters. Goudie was responsible for accounts A to H. This, of course, included Mr Hudson.

One member of the gang who engineered the blackmail and robbing of Goudie escaped. Goudie's misfortune was that having "borrowed" £100 from the Bank he put it on a horse which won at eight to one. Eldorado beckoned. It was so easy — and so fatal....

From my own experience I found that the radio play was a stepping stone to the TV play and this in turn was an avenue that led to the profitable but unpredictable world of films.

The new author cannot afford, unless his early books are exceptionally successful, to ignore the drama field. A radio play does not take more than a month to write, perhaps less, and the returns on the original showing and, possibly with repeats and foreign rights, may bring in income over a period; though the new writer can only be sure of the price he will be paid as stipulated by his contract.

A friend, reading this chapter, said: "Yes, but you had insinuated yourself into the drama writing world. You knew a number of writers and were able to borrow scripts from which you gleaned all the clues to this specialised branch of writing. A new writer might know no-one who could help him."

I am afraid this is one of those obstacles that just has to be overcome by the writer himself. In another chapter I explore the possibilities of the new writer creating a public image that will certainly lead to invitations to take part in programmes on the BBC and commercial channels. And this in turn will introduce him to the studio people, the writers, directors, managers and others. The difficulty is not insuperable. Opportunities will present themselves. By hook or by crook he has to get these scripts for they hold the key to his future as a drama writer. The lesson seems to be that the determined man or woman is not excluded for too long. This section of the writing world may be tough but the people in it are often surprisingly helpful.

I have not dealt with the glittering world of the stage play because so many good plays appear after an interval in book form. There is nothing like seeing a play with increasing understanding and observation to give the new writer the techniques he seeks.

Finally, the new writer seeking to penetrate the world of radio, television and films should not fail to consult the factual information given in the *Writers' and Artists' Year book* under the heading Theatre, Radio and TV. The advice on marketing is especially valuable as is the section on sales abroad, including the United States.

CHAPTER 9

Agents, Copyright and Defamation

The question of whether the new writer does well to employ an agent is a vexed one. For authors who live in or near either London or New York it may well be that the author himself, who is closer to and more concerned with his own promotion as a writer than any agent can be, is well able to promote his own books. It may also depend on the kind of career he intends to pursue. If he is a quiet author just writing at home he will gather few contacts and the good agent may well be worth employing. If he is of the extrovert type who exploits his books to get his name known on television and radio and in contentious public debate, he will himself make a lot of contacts at home and abroad and out of these he may be able to forge his way to popularity and success more effectively than any agent is able to do for him, bearing in mind that the agent may have fifty or even two hundred clients to attend to. In "Show Business" it is believed that artists and actors have to become identified by the public in order to create a demand for their services. Books by "well-known" authors tend to sell better than those written by writers whom the public have never heard of.

There is a compromise situation where an author, believing he has an absolute winner, either as a package "property" or as a book, may approach an agent to exploit it. Agents do not favour this kind of limited relationship but if they, too, see a brilliant and viable idea capable of wide exploitation, the money involved may well overcome their natural resentment. Moreover, they calculate perhaps that if they make a success of the project the author may change his mind and employ them permanently.

It is well to bear in mind that the agent is exactly what the term implies, namely, an agent for the author who is the principal. Agents usually deduct their commission on monies coming to them on the way to the author. With regard to money paid to the author arising out of introductions made by the agent, the author should remit the commission without delay or argument. It is always distressing to have to pay out, but if, as is usually the case, the agent is straight with the author, the author owes it to the agent to be prompt in any money matters that may be in the agent's favour. A list of reputable agents in Britain and overseas is in the *Writers' and Artists' Year Book* and some big agents have representation in various countries.

Copyright is the author's title to his work. No registration is needed. When the work is complete he merely stamps it with a large "C" (the accepted abbreviation for copyright) and his name. It is then his copyright.

The major and essential rule for the author is never to part with your copyright. You may sell "rights", yes, but the copyright should always be yours.

Copyright has a long history. The description following, published nearly a century ago, shows a developing law. "Copy" which started as a privilege was becoming a right.

"Copyright, or, as it was formerly termed, Copy, has been defined by Lord Mansfield 'to signify an incorporeal right to the sole printing and publishing of somewhat intellectual, communicated by letters'. By this 'somewhat intellectual' is to be understood something proceeding from the mind of the person by whom, or through whom, such a right is claimable. Translations, and notes and additions to existing works, are similarly protected. Further, a right of copy attaches to the authors of ideas expressed by other symbols as well as letters — to musical composers for example.

"It has been supposed that a common-law right of copy existed in England previously to any statute on the subject. But it is unimportant whether this was so or not, for the statutes as to copyright have put an end to perpetual copyright, if it ever existed.

"The universities of Cambridge and Oxford obtained from Parliament, in the year 1775, an Act for enabling those two universities in England, the four universities in Scotland, and the several colleges of Eton, Westminster and Winchester to hold in perpetuity their copyright in books given or bequeathed to the said universities and colleges for the advancement of useful learning and other purposes of education. A similar protection is extended to the University of Dublin by 41 Geo.III c. 107.

"The Act 5 & 6 Vict.c.45 (Lord Mahon's Act), entitled 'an Act to amend the Law of Copyright' and having for its preamble 'Whereas it is expedient to amend the law relating to copyright, and to afford greater encouragement to the production of literary works of lasting benefit to the world', is the Act which now regulates literary property. It enacts that, in every book published in the lifetime of the author, after the passing of the Act (1st July 1842) the author and his assigns shall have copyright for the term of the author's life and for seven years after his death."

We have come a long way since then in two directions. Firstly, the laws on international copyright are slowly assuming some kind of cohesion and similarity, though there are still countries with no copyright law and others who constantly and flagrantly defy existing laws on their statute books. Secondly, the period of copyright in Britain has been extended so that now copyright — the author's title to his work — is usually for his life and for fifty years from the end of the calendar year in which he died. Publishers and magazines sometimes seek to acquire copyright in a book on publication or serialisation, but reputable publishers will not do this as the author's right to title is generally acknowledged.

Libel is so important to authors, publishers and printers of a book that I make no apology for going into the matter fairly fully. We use the generic term defamation to cover both libel — recorded defamation — and slander which is spoken defamation. The injured party, of course, is anyone whose reputation is maligned. It is not necessary for the author to intend to malign the victim if in fact he does so.

Slander is a much less serious "tort" than libel and we need not deal with it here. Libel is so serious because damages — not being a question of law to be decided by the judge — are determined by the jury who sometimes return a verdict that entails the payment of frightening and crippling amounts.

There is no way, in a serious case, of telling whether the damages will be £5,000 or £50,000 and whether legal costs will also be awarded to the Plaintiff if he wins his case. Libel cases often appear to hover on a legal borderline so that appeals are frequent and this adds to the already exorbitant costs involved.

So we are dealing with an aspect of the writing profession that may indeed land the author, his publisher and his printer in deep trouble. For this reason the larger publishing firms usually employ a law firm specialising in defamation which relieves the publisher and author of some anxiety but of no liability. The consulted lawyers may be wrong.

The law of England on libel has been grim from the beginning. I quote a Victorian authority:

> "LIBEL (from the Latin *libellus*, a little book) is a malicious defamation, expressed either in writing or by signs, pictures etc. tending either to blacken the memory of one who is dead, or the representation of one who is alive, and thereby exposing him to public hatred, contempt, or ridicule. This species of defamation is usually termed 'written scandal' and it is generally treated as more serious mode of defamation than SLANDER.
>
> "Whatever written words tend to render a man ridiculous or to lower him in the estimation of the world, amount to a libel, although the very same expressions, if spoken, would not have been slander or defamation in the legal sense of these words. To complete the offence publication is necessary. The mere writing of defamatory matter without publication is not an offence punishable by law; but if a libel in a man's handwriting is found, the proof is thrown upon him to show that he did not also publish it."

The old law has been much amended. Today, broadly, this is the main outline of the law.
1. Libel is a written (or other permanent reproduction) of material injurious to a man's reputation or exposing him to hatred, ridicule or contempt.
2. The Plaintiff need not show "specific" damage. Damage may be inferred from the nature of the libel.
3. The libelled party may bring a civil or a criminal action.

4. In civil cases there must always be "publication" to some person or persons other than the Plaintiff.
5. In a civil action the Plaintiff will lose his case if the author of the libel can prove that the statements made are true. This does not apply in a criminal case.
6. There are a variety of defences to an action for libel. One is privilege as when an employer is recommending an employee, another is the Statute of Limitations which lays down that any action must commence within six years. Newspapers have several defences of which "fair comment on a matter of public interest" is the most common.
7. By an Act of 1952 anyone who innocently published a libel made by another person may make an offer of compensation instead of "damages". This is usually linked with an agreed apology and an undertaking not to repeat the offence.

All this is legalistic but, I think, well worth the study of the author. At least he realises what dangerous ground he is treading if he dips his pen in venom. But I should attempt to indicate some guideline that would avoid libel for the author altogether in simple layman's terms. Perhaps the best answer — by no means comprehensive — is that, although you may indulge in any amount of fair criticism of public men, you must not malign the private lives of men, public or private, or, if you do, be quite sure that every word you write is not only true but can be proved to be true. And never malign a man "in the way of his trade or profession" unless you are prepared to face especially heavy damages in the event of a successful suit being brought against you.

Finally, my own personal experience in managing a highly controversial advertising campaign for three years without having a single libel action brought against the authors of the advertisement, proved the value of one rule. *Read carefully and, when in doubt, cut.*

CHAPTER 10

Foreign Markets

The prestige of British writers is high abroad. In Europe, in the thirty-five Commonwealth countries and in America, as well as in Africa and in the Far East, including South-East Asia, there is a constant demand for British books.

However, there are broad differences and distinctions arising out of the history of the country concerned, the matter of language, for instance. In the United States, in spite of the very large immigrant minorities, by a magnificent achievement of assimilation, English is spoken and read by almost the entire literate population. In the Commonwealth English is either the first language, as in Canada, Australia, New Zealand and Tasmania, or the second language as in India and Pakistan. English is also the dual language — with Afrikaans — in South Africa. In independent Thailand English is the second language as it is in Malaysia. In all the former black colonies of Britain in Africa, now independent, English is the second language. Hongkong is the key to China.

Thus a vast market opens out to the English-speaking author. The chief exceptions to the rule are the former French colonies in Africa, including Morocco, and a large number of lesser states, now independent. The other great exception is the former Spanish empire, which covers virtually the whole of South and Central America with the exception of Brazil, an important market, where Portuguese is spoken.

However, in many countries such as Brazil and dual language Switzerland, as well as in Scandinavia, there is a demand for British books. If I may again give a personal example, I wrote a straight crime book on famous murders. To my surprise and delight a Brazilian publisher requested the right to publish the book in Portuguese which he did very well with a dust-jacket more arresting than the one we had thought up in London. This was followed by a request for permission to base a course of lectures at the premier University of Brazil on the cases covered by *Murder Parade* and the comments in that book on crime and punishment, the prison system, parole, crime and insanity, and crime and society. The request came from a very distinguished professor who was delivering a course of lectures on these topics.

Despite the Anglo-American campaign, for that is what it amounts to, to make the entire world speak English — Esperanto is apparently a non-starter — certain countries are obdurate. The French cling tenaciously to their own tongue as do the Italians, the Spanish, the Russians and the Chinese. Many Japanese, however, now speak and even read some English.

The custom is for the foreign publisher in his contract to include the right to translate "the work" into his own and possibly other languages. As the not inconsiderable cost of translation falls on the publisher and not the author, the writer has no cause to complain. It is delightful to see one's books with foreign covers and often new titles. I have never got bored by these transformations. *The Golden Orchid* has become *La Guerre de l'Orchidée* when published by a Paris firm. *Murder Parade,* published by the Instituicao Brasleira de Difusao Cultural S.A. in São Paulo, became *Crimes en Désfile. The Great Assassins,* when published by the Arco Publishing Company in New York, retained its title but its restrained British cover was replaced by a man aiming a gun straight through your eyes and the "blurb" gave an appropriate American slant: "The chilling true stories behind twenty infamous assassinations, including the Kennedy brothers and Martin Luther King."

Although up to now British business has proceeded on the principle that "all the top men abroad" speak English (and like to be given the opportunity to practise it) perhaps the time is approaching, or is long overdue, when in correspondence we might consider writing in French, German or whatever. Translators are easy to come by. I have recently been stymied by one or two German publishers who have written to me in German. I realised that my surprise and well-concealed resentment was wholly unjustified — and replied in English. But a wind of change is blowing and we may have to consider mending our ways.

Some countries have a far larger market than one would

suspect. The sale of British books, both popular, classical, and technical, in South Africa is very large and valuable. I was stunned on a recent visit to Durban to find twenty-eight of my forty books in the excellently run public library.

The new author should therefore be aware of the great opportunities presented by world markets from the start. I only woke up to it after I had been writing for five years. We British have a deeply entrenched insularity. I think this would not apply to nearly the same extent with the new intake of young authors whose views are the liberal, pragmatic views of the "in" generation.

If, as I believe he should, the new author does decide to look into this question of foreign markets for his books as soon as his first book is published and before his second, I suggest the following possible procedures for getting in touch with overseas publishers in order to supplement the efforts made by your Publisher.

1. Acquire twenty copies of your book at the reduced price from your Publisher (in addition to the six free copies for your file and personal friends).
2. Post these to twenty leading publishers in other countries, together with some favourable press clippings from *The Telegraph* and *The Guardian*, as well as a synopsis of your next book. And perhaps also *New York Times* etc. clippings.
3. State frankly that you are approaching them because they are leading publishers in the country concerned and state that you have made no other approach.
4. If you do not employ an agent say so and indicate that any business can be done with you direct, or through your Publisher.
5. In this kind of approach in my opinion it is necessary to write your letter in their language or, if you like, in that language with an English copy.
6. Realise that you are adopting an unusual procedure that I myself and some of my writing friends have found effective. Of course, it costs something in postage, but the investment initially in the writing business is so small that this modest output may well be a very good extra investment.

A large number of leading authors believe that the employment of an agent to exploit the foreign market is essential. I am not convinced, but their success seems to be a good argument in the agents' favour. My own feeling is that small agents are apt to be passed over by the great foreign publishing houses and the most prestigious agents sometimes seem to have very little time for an "unknown" author joining their list. I hope that this is not so. Perhaps, after all, we should expect this. The big man who smells of sweet success gets the best restaurant table. It is the way of the world. When the lady who helps with my manuscripts ordered some new notepaper for me at a local printer who had, he said, a backlog of orders, the saleswoman asked if I was "a celebrity". Steeling herself to the challenge the answer she gave was "Yes, haven't you heard of him?" A brave overstatement but it did the trick. Our small order was promoted to celebrity status for speedy delivery.

In the course of more unconventional work, which may come to you for the simple reason that you are in a certain country, never forget the International Press Agencies. An example: I was in Athens with my wife doing research for a non-political tourist book, one of the "Magnet Books", written at the request of the government concerned to attract tourists world-wide. I had a message at the Grande Bretagne Hotel that the Dictator, no less, would like to meet me. Next morning an Aide would call to take me to the presence. The Aide was punctual and explained: "The Prime Minister has been very badly treated by foreign journalists recently. As you are an author, already interested in our country, he invites you to interview him and will answer any questions you care to put."

So it was arranged. I asked all the questions, including the tricky ones about alleged police brutality and prison torture. We both signed the interview as authentic. Next day, our research mission concluded, we returned to England and the following day I sold the interview to the best-known Press Agency in London, who in turn used it in over fifty outlets in the United States, including newspapers, broadcasting and television.

This is an off-shoot of the foreign market that may well arise when you are travelling and I suggest you make contact with at least one such agency before you go. Authors who travel a lot sometimes are given rare opportunities. Breakfasting at the Khartoum Hotel one morning we were called to the telephone. It was the *Daily Mail*. Would I join the plane of the Emperor of Ethiopa which was touching down at Khartoum on its way to take the Emperor to Addis Ababa to quell a revolution?

It was to be a memorable occasion. Flying into Eritrea, the Emperor took a large helicopter, landing in the main square of his capital. There was a huge crowd— standing. The rebels were in charge of the Palace and the capital. The Lion of Judah spoke from a raised platform erected by the rebels to address their supporters. He made a sign. To the horror of the rebellious Army Officers the crowd — submitting to immemorial custom— sank to their knees. It was all over. The Emperor returned to his Palace.

Whatever happened to the rebellious Army Officers?

The term "foreign markets" in the book trade may include some bizarre situations, but traditionally Englishmen have been able to cope with these. In fact, it was touch and go.

I hope this chapter has persuaded you that you should look into the business to be done with your books all over the world. Most countries are now not more than two days away. Often it is not even necessary to leave London or New York — if you live there — to make your contacts.

Most of the largest foreign publishers have an office in London. There is also a large Press Corps from over thirty countries. Recently I sold three feature articles in Africa without leaving London. The newspaper concerned delegated all negotiations — and payment — to their London Office. I followed my usual procedure of making delivery just before, and not just after, the deadline. That evening the features were rushed to Heathrow in time to catch the night plane. Next afternoon they had arrived.

Certainly, it will take time before a new author can benefit from all the diverse opportunities I have dealt with in this chapter, but I hope that by making himself familiar with the chief foreign markets at an early stage in his career he will reap a continuing benefit that otherwise he might miss.

The author does not merely need to write carefully and well, to research, to produce a synopsis of each work. He needs to explore and exploit all aspects of the writing profession and of these, the foreign markets for his books, for subsidiary rights and even for his freelance journalism, form a most important part.

CHAPTER 11

Tourism and Travel Books

Travel books are not a promising field for the new author. For some reason they are not fashionable. A century ago they were devoured by an eager public perhaps because there was still unexplored territory — and people whose customs were so bizarre as to be good reading in themselves. Today, when one is likely to meet a BBC camera team in the Khyber Pass, or an intrepid American group of agricultural experts on the border between Thailand and the Shan states, the lustre seems to have gone out of travel books. But there are always exceptions, tales so arresting that no publisher can resist them.

Usually, the book meeting with success in this area either describes Victorian travel — Alan Moorhead's superb *White Nile* is an example — or a book such as Lawrence Durrell's *Bitter Lemons* about a more recent period, set in Cyprus but before the division of the island between Turks and Greeks.

The true travel book is factual but a number of great historical novels satisfy the same curiosity, such as *The Lacquer Lady*, the magic recreation of the Court of the last Burmese King, *Siamese White*, the brilliant story of an interloper in Old Siam. These are exceptional books that would break any barriers. The pace and convenience of travel may have killed the element of surprise in the true travel book. In 1930 Bangkok was six weeks from London by ship, calling at British ports only until reaching independent Siam. Today, the same journey takes eighteen hours by Jumbo Jet.

Certainly, I would not dissuade any new writer who has travelled uniquely to write a travel book, but it is only right to point out the difficulties of this type of book for both publisher and author.

Tourism is another matter. Tourism is the biggest "growth industry" in the world. Tourism is indeed a communications business. It can only continue to increase by making contact with an ever larger public. And this in turn can only be done either by advertising or by tourist books. The advantage of a tourist book about a particular country is that it is durable, it is in the libraries, and it is not the promotion of the country concerned but of an independent author who has adopted this field of writing and specialised in it. It is an area of the writing profession that includes attractive "fringe benefits" and a fair rate of royalties on the book itself.

Fifteen years ago my wife suggested to me that, as we liked to travel in the sun, especially during January and February, it should be possible to combine this with writing. From her suggestion I gave the name "Magnet Books" to the tourist books I have written since I started in this field. A magnet book was and is a book "that describes the tourist attractions of the country concerned favourably but accurately with the objective of attracting more tourists to the country."

I found that many governments, through their Departments of Tourism, were eager to have a book of this kind and would invite myself and my wife (who took the photographs) as guests for one or two months to complete our research on the spot. The arrangement included return air fares for us both, usually by the national airline of the country concerned. The financial side of the operation suited both parties. As the Government concerned often owned hotels and other accommodation as well as its airline, the payments were largely a matter of transferring money from one Government account to another. As far as we were concerned, we were enabled to do the research and take the photographs in the best possible way, for as Government guests we had no problems, the path was always smooth and it was in the interest of both the tourist authorities and ourselves that all should go well.

Sometimes the Government would place an order for the book with our publishers at the time of signing the Publisher-Author contract. This enabled them to receive a discount of 33.3% on the booksellers' price. Some Governments preferred to place an order after publication. It is sometimes suggested that a sponsored book is not the work of an independent author. This is quite untrue. The avowed object of such a book is to "sell" the tourist attractions of the

77

country. In order that this may be achieved the book has to be an honest book or it defeats its purpose. Tourist books should not indulge in any politics. Tourism has nothing to do with ideology. The tourist, whatever race, colour, or religion, is welcome as a tourist. He is welcome because he comes, leaves his travellers' cheques behind, and goes. He is the perfect paying guest, especially to countries chronically short of foreign exchange.

When we conceived the idea of the "magnet book" I sought a country not too large, friendly in its relations with my own, in which most of the officials would speak English as well as their own language. I chose Jordan. It was a most happy choice. For the first and last time we paid our expenses and put up at the modest Continental Hotel in Amman. After a week, meeting agreeable Ministers who said: "Has His Majesty received you yet?" King Hussein called me to the Palace. He asked what I proposed to do in Jordan? I told him. He agreed. From that moment we were the guests of the Jordan Government. Fifteen years later, returning briefly to Jordan, I was met at the airport by an official who told me: "You are staying at the Intercontinental as the guest of the Palace." This was totally unexpected — but typical of a generous man who does not forget.

I suppose because we started with the Hashemite Kingdom of Jordan, in the years that followed we tended to specialise in the Islamic world, though I spoke no Arabic. In the next two or three years I may well retire from this part of the writing craft, confining myself to one book a year at home. If this happens, someone will be able to take my place. For the benefit of new writers who might be attracted by the tourist book as I have described it, may I explain that each book has to be tailored to the country being approached. Without a thoughtful and careful approach, success is unlikely. It is true that Christian countries have something in common, as do Moslem countries. But each country regards itself rightly as being different from its neighbours. It is in discovering the difference and making this the theme of the book that the secret of success lies.

May I give some short examples. My introduction to *Modern Saudi Arabia*, which sold out ten thousand copies on publication, contains these passages.

I asked the Saudi Government in Riyadh whether I might come to Saudi Arabia to write a book with a definite theme. That theme was: That the evolution and extremely rapid progress of Saudi Arabia has been and is being achieved within the framework of Islam and indeed sustained and fortified by the Islamic way of life.

This seemed to me to be essentially what made Saudi Arabia different from her Arab neighbours. All Arab states are embracing modern technology, a field in which they got left behind during the centuries of Ottoman domination. But in most of these states the advance into a new scientific materialism has been accompanied by some corrosion of faith. One is aware of this all the time. Ramadan is not so strictly observed, the other basic laws of Islam are observed only if the rush of 'modern life' allows time for such devotions.

In Saudi Arabia it seemed to me that the Islamic way of life was as strong today as it was during the life of Mohammed. It impregnated the whole structure of government. The Constitution of the state was the Koran which gave the country its laws and its deterrents. Islam was all. But because the Moslem faith is one of dignity, independence and courage, that faith was itself giving men the confidence to enter a new world with success."

It was this approach that made my two visits to Riyadh so valuable and rewarding.

The foreword to my book on Jordan — now in urgent need of revision after fifteen turbulent years of change — struck the note for my approach to Jordan.

The Hashemite Kingdom of Jordan is one of the newest and most fascinating states of the Near East.

Jordan comprises nearly all the Holy Land, and, maintained within her borders, are spectacular examples of Roman, Greek and Byzantine civilization. No writer on Jordan could ignore this lineage and tradition, nor is it ignored by the Jordan Government today.

The Roman city of Jarash is carefully preserved in its original grandeur and dignity; while in a recent Christmas broadcast to his people, King Hussein said: 'We look upon it as our duty to preserve and maintain the holy places of Christendom.'

In spite of these deep and proud roots I have called this book *Modern Jordan* and kept within the terms of reference this title implies, because it is the kingdom of Jordan today that is important to us all, whether we are statesmen, diplomats, teachers, students or the general public.

I ask the reader to co-operate with me in two ways. First to remember that we are describing a Moslem country with attitudes and traditions different from our own. The followers of the Prophet, on the whole, have a greater regard for dignity, gratitude, hospitality, courage and reputation in day-to-day life than we have in the West, if only because they are nearer to a nomadic natural life in which these qualities had more immediate significance. It is equally true that Near Eastern people do not attach the importance to scientific invention and material wealth that we do. This gulf between the philosophy of the Near East and the West accounts for the difficulties and misunderstandings that arise from time to time, even when the West is trying to aid the East.

The second point I would ask you to bear in mind is that the world appears quite different if looked at from Amman or Jerusalem, than it does if we are viewing it from Washington, London, Bonn or Paris.

I do not believe it is possible to convey the feeling, atmosphere and tradition of a nation, as well as report the facts, unless one is prepared to write as if looking out on the world from within the country itself. And I have written this book, in so far as I am able, looking out of a Jordanian window on the world."

In the case of *An Invitation to South Africa* I studiously avoided any political implications and, because tourists often have to travel great distances by sea or air to reach the Republic, I concentrated on the genuine attractions of South African tourism for those who believe that tourism and politics should not be mixed.

The urge to take a holiday is as old as nomadic man, as new as the jet age. What everyone is looking for is somewhere different. There is nothing wrong with home, but it is a great place to come back to. After being anchored for so long, the ship must sail away. The man, the woman and the children must pack and go on a voyage of discovery, or in simpler terms, have a holiday. Change is the most essential ingredient of a holiday. As Sir Winston Churchill pointed out to his overworked staff: 'All you need is a change. We're going to Washington next week.'

South Africa represents to Europeans and Americans the greatest possible change. It is a country with many races, with several climates, with a great choice of food and wine, with abundant wild life, with some of the best entertainment in the world, a country with space and great contrasts where today is more important than yesterday and tomorrow more important than today, a rich country with a limitless future where the hotels are superb, the roads excellent — a motorist's paradise — and where the people welcome the visitor openly and generously.

This description is enthusiastic but true. South Africa is a fabulous tourist country with a variety of good climates.

All the magnet books were not directed solely to tourism. Saudi Arabia for instance — apart from the half million pilgrims who visit Mecca during Ramadan — has few tourists though many business visitors. So the book describes Saudi Arabia to the world in general as well as to the visitor in particular.

Bearing in mind the importance of assessing each country's

individuality, the format of the book follows a logical sequence. This is done most effectively by the author taking his reader on a conducted tour of the country, visiting and appreciating with intelligence the great cities, the historic treasures, sporting events, and the life of the place including accommodation, food, wine, climate and places of entertainment.

For instance, in *Visiting Egypt* the first six chapters are entitled:

1. Welcome to Egypt.
2. Expeditions from Cairo
3. Up the Nile to Abu Simbel
4. Helwan and Alexandria
5. The Road to El Alamein and Gianaclis
6. More of Cairo — and Sinai.

And the Appendix, an important feature, covered the following:

Currency Regulations
Weather Statistics
List of Museums and Notable Monuments
Hotels and Nightclubs
Embassies and Consular Establishments

On the cover of *Visiting Egypt*, in colour, is a photograph of the Sphinx which, without words, instantly identifies the book with Egypt. But this photograph was more than that. We took the photo from an unusual angle, from the side, looking up. The battered nose caused by one of Napoleon's cannon dominates the face of the Sphinx, seen — not as inscrutable — but as fiercely resentful. Perhaps suggesting that Egyptians do not like being bullied.

Freak photographs that bring a totally unexpected reward can and do occur. In the Sudan, returning from Baka-ruda one hundred and fifty miles across the desert from Khartoum and some ten miles short of the city, we saw quite a large Sudanese village ahead on the right of the track. We could not believe it. My wife took a photograph. On being developed it showed the village as we had seen it. But on that day, after taking the picture, less than a mile further on the entire illusion had disappeared. The following week we repeated this with the conventional mirage scene of water and palm trees. Again this vanished on being approached but appeared distinctively and sharply on the negative and print.

The Magnet book, which I came to regard as my special preserve, brought us great interest and happiness. We visited over twenty countries altogether, some of which gave unexpected results. Two visits to Greece led to my being invited to join a four-man delegation of MPs to report on Greek elections. A visit to Tehran prompted a fabulous party given by the late King Faisal in London when he was guarded by two giant Nubians whose duty it was to throw themselves on any assailant. Our first visit to Jordan resulted in kindness shown us for twenty years by King Hussein. We were the first writers to visit Turkish Cyprus after the North of the island had been occupied by Turkey. In the Khyber Pass we bargained for about an hour to buy two lamb rugs and reduced the asking price by half, only to find that identical rugs were being sold more cheaply in Hove, Sussex. We had the experience of meeting President Nasser, a natural hero, handsome, dominating, a Pharaoh of the people. It was all worth while.

So the tourist book is a valuable and ever-growing part of the writing profession. And it has other advantages. Tourism does nothing but good. The more people travel in countries other than their own, the more they will understand and appreciate the customs, manners and even aspirations of all classes and all colours. Writing tourist books one is very much on the side of the angels.

Perhaps I may be allowed to give one tip to any writer who likes the idea of writing magnet books— there is no copyright in titles — and that is: Aim high.

On the face of it the writing and publication of a book on any aspect of national life, including tourism, is not too important a matter in the context of Government affairs. But, in fact, because the book may, for better or worse, affect the country's "image" world-wide, it is of much more concern to the Authorities than one might suppose. It is therefore likely that final approval for the project will be sought high up in the hierarchy. There are two dangers in becoming involved too low down the ladder. The first is that the man on whose desk the proposal rests may, for some unrevealed reason, take a dislike to the project. He may think his cousin, a local author, would do the job much better, in which case he will take a copy of the synopsis and ensure that if the proposal reaches the Minister at all, it will be accompanied by an adverse recommendation.

The second danger is that, having been dealt with at a certain conventional level, those above may conclude that you are happy to negotiate at this level which is a straight road to failure. I am a great believer in "unusual channels" when it comes to dealing with Governments in Southern Europe, the Middle East or the Far East. By the same token I have always asked for first-class air tickets, finding out by experience that this request did much more than provide us with comfortable passages (and champagne). It separated the author from the journalist, that intrepid tribe who have to obtain a story which sometimes the Authorities have no intention of revealing. Authors would not be there unless they had been invited. The guest is a privileged person and one needs all the help and special treatment one can obtain to overcome the hard labour of some weeks of research.

One can so easily get bogged down among Under-Secretaries and even Secretaries to important persons. On the other hand Secretaries can be useful. On a recent trip to Jordan during a visit by the Sultan of Oman which occupied the King's time, it was entirely due to the kindness of a young British secretary in Prince Hassan's office that I was able to meet the King and his brother on Jordanian Independence Day when there was a three mile long Military Parade.

To anyone who decides to pursue the tourist trail I wish them well and promise them that, if they are able to achieve results, they will enjoy meeting men of power as well as a great many ordinary people, lawyers, politicians, soldiers, shopkeepers and the farmers and workers who are the backbone of it all. Never miss the doctors. I had one of the most entertaining evenings of my life dining with two young Egyptian doctors in a Cairo Lunatic Asylum.

The Tourist book in the terms I have described has obtained itself a niche in some of the Publishers lists but is still regarded as a minor category of the writing profession. I predict that in the next decade it will grow rapidly. Still in its infancy, it is just the kind of business that new writers could profitably exploit.

CHAPTER 12

Language and the Cultural Heritage

There is often misunderstanding concerning the interesting question of the author's attitude towards money. The professional author who lives by his writing has to be concerned with his annual income. Money is the lash that drives him to work with regularity and dedication. There is nothing wrong with this. Shakespeare, that perennial example, worked much harder when he was in immediate need of money than he did during an affluent spell when he was apt to enjoy himself at the expense of his business. We call writing a business but of course it is more than a business. It is creative. It is original. It is the child of the author's head and heart. An author will bargain with his Publisher but when the bargain has been struck the amount of money involved will not affect the quality of the work, for the author has to write as well as he can. There is something that drives him to do this. If he descends to careless substandard writing he feels unhappy and forced to start again, giving the best that is in him to the task that is in hand.

The fact that authorship is both a vocation and a livelihood makes it essential that the new author should acquaint himself with the origin and development of the English language, as well as with the national culture which authors did much to create and promote, a culture which was derived from many sources and, in the form of literature, achieved great influence in the English-speaking world and in those countries which formed part of the British Empire.

Many authors, but by no means all, will come to writing already familiar with the roots and growth of the English language and English literature, so it may be appropriate to remind new authors at least of the outline of both these subjects.

The English language was originally formed from the languages spoken by various tribes from the North of Germany who settled in this country in the 5th and 6th centuries. The principal of these were the Jutes, the Saxons and the Angles. The aboriginal Britons were driven into the mountainous parts to the West where their language, Welsh, still flourishes. At subsequent periods English received additions from the Danish, Greek, Latin and French languages and it is to this long period of blending and reinforcement that we owe the wonderful variety, vigour and range of twentieth century English.

Although there are said to be some forty thousand words in the English language, common literary English, even today, probably does not exceed ten thousand words and in ordinary conversation not more than five thousand words are used. At the bottom of the scale a large number of "uneducated" people manage to lead happy and productive lives using about one thousand words to express themselves. This is so worldwide. A Chinese multi-millionaire of my acquaintance could neither read nor write.

We have a large collection of prose and poetry in the ancient English form — the *English Chronicle*, the translations made or edited by King Alfred, the homilies and writings of Abbot Aelfric, as well as the verse of Beowulf.

The Norman invasion brought in French modes of thought and versification, like those of the Troubadours, rhyming and metrical, rather than alliterative like the Norse and Anglo-Saxon poems. And the vocabulary was enriched and altered by the introduction of French — Latin words. But the basis of the language among the people, as opposed to the Court and the upper classes, still continued to be Low German. A period of transition led through Robert of Gloucester, William Langley and others to the culmination of a true Middle English in the grand prose of Wickliffe and the yet grander verse of Chaucer, recognised as the father of modern English literature.

Old English was related to the Indo-European or Aryan languages which included Indian as Sanskrit, Persian as Zend, Slavonic as Russian, Celtic as Gaelic, Greco-Latin as Greek and Gothic as German.

French was brought over by the Normans at the time of the Norman Conquest, but even during the previous reign of the Confessor, it had become the Court language as Edward had spent his youth abroad and was French rather than English in his tastes.

The French language, apart from being a direct source of much modern English, also acted as a filter for innumerable Latin words. For instance, the names of the Roman stations and camps such as Doncaster; the ecclesiastical terms of the English conversion — chalice, candle, cloister, mass, minster and monk. There were direct importations of Latin by the scholars of the Renaissance and men of science over the centuries.

Greek words in the English language are almost exclusively literary having been introduced by churchmen and scholars. The nouns usually retained their own plurals as is so often the case in imperfectly naturalised words. We say phenomena, automata, and dogmata which has now become completely integrated as dogma.

There is a minor but most interesting source of English which is the Norse element brought over by the Danish conquerors and filtering from East Anglia and Northumbria into common speech. It is from this source that the Manx language is derived, a language still spoken by the country people within the present century but today only kept alive by the Manx Language Society and by the fact that the laws of Tynwald are read in Manx once a year on Tynwald Day.

Perhaps the most diverting and diverse additions to the English language have come to us through the contacts made by the English adventurers during the last five hundred years and later by the extraordinary creation of a British Empire containing some thirty-five foreign nations, each with their own cultural heritage and language. Some of the foreign importations go back much earlier than this, for instance Hebrew gives us Bible terms as in ephod, cherub and seraph; Arabic terms of lore, usually regarded as secret, gave us algebra, alchemy, talisman, cipher and zero. Persian has sent us paradise and several dyes such as scarlet, azure and lilac. Turkish has given us scimitar, pasha and sultan. Our word gong is, of course, Chinese; our bantam and sago are Malay; our calico, chintz, curry and muslin are Indian; taboo and tatoo are from the Pacific; tobacco, potato, maize and hurricane are, as one might expect, West Indian in origin. Squaw and wigwam come from the "Red Indians". Hammock is South American while from Italy we received guerilla, pantaloon and gazette. Spanish provides us with cocoa and chocolate, mosquito, negro, punctillo and alligator. Finally Portuguese presented us with marmalade, caste and coconut while the Dutch contributed yacht, sloop and buoy.

The ramifications are, of course, endless and quite impossible to explore completely in a book of this kind but I cannot resist mentioning the curious little group of words derived from the names of towns, for instance cherry (Gerasus), currant (Corinth), damson (Damascus), guinea (Guinea gold), peach (Persia) (persica), parchment (Pergamus), and spaniel (Spain).

We exploit and adapt modern English without much regard to the source of fundamental meaning of words. There is a great exchange of vocabulary between Britain and the United States and between France and England. However, the old-fashioned connoisseur of words has perhaps been hurried off the modern literary scene. We no longer get Doctor Johnson's sudden exclamation of anger at a dull and rude jest: "Sir, it has not wit enough to keep it sweet;" which, as he saw Boswell noting down the epigram, he corrected by the phrase "to preserve it from putrefaction," according to his usual habit of Latinizing the nervous English tongue.

The new author, as he becomes immersed in his craft, will naturally and automatically acquire a mastery of words and a greatly extended vocabulary. He will also tend to use words more correctly because he will have taken the trouble to assure himself of their exact meaning which is often quite obvious when we know their root. For instance, the word innuendo means an oblique hint, the root being *innuere*, to nod. Curiously enough, the lawyers, precise as ever, use the word as referring to that part of their written pleading which expresses the real meaning of defamatory words and the words "meaning thereby" are used as common form followed by the exact interpretation which the Plaintiff gives to the words of which he complains. Certain words tend to lose their original strict meaning. For instance, alibi essentially means "I was not there. I was somewhere else." It is, of course, common for people accused of committing a certain crime at a certain place to use this plea, but today alibi is commonly used to signify an excuse in general terms. Such changes are always resisted by the purists but a language should never allow a dead hand to strangle it and a constantly changing and growing language is a vital and vigorous one indicative of a vital and vigorous people who use it.

Occasionally, there are misuses of English that are regrettable even though their use may be irresistable. When Mr Harold Macmillan was being questioned by a journalist on the "Rhodesian problem", he gently pointed out that the situation in Rhodesia was not a problem. It was a "situation" — calling for certain measures which might or might not improve that situation. A problem was something capable of precise definition and solution — *quod erat demonstrandum*. It is as well that occasionally our lax use of our language should be questioned by those who still have a respect for the right use of words.

When the English language is regarded in its concrete form as English literature the subject is vast and it is only possible to indicate salient points in the changing pattern of time. Two very ancient English verse have come down to us. One is the Exeter Book given as a valuable relic by Leofric, Bishop of Exeter, to his Cathedral about 1050. The other is the Vercelli Book discovered in Italy in 1823 but certainly of 8th century origin.

Alfred the Great gave a new direction to English literature. With a limited knowledge of Latin it was his hobby and life-long task to translate Bede's *Ecclesiastical History* and half-a-dozen other works. Towards the end of his life he wrote the famous *English Chronicle*.

The change to the poems of Chaucer came like a burst of sunlight to the literary scene. His fine taste and his wonderful power of sketching character joined to a command of language made Chaucer unknowingly the founder of our modern English language and our literature. English literature has often had a kingly connection. James I was described as "The best poet among kings, the best king among poets." During his long captivity in England he caught the English vein and in his own style sung some fine songs. By this time alliteration, which had been at the core of the oldest English verse, had almost vanished and rhyming had taken its place. Centuries later Swinbourne was to use alliteration with great effect but it would now be regarded as dated and unfashionable.

Malory's *Mort d'Arthur* was one of the first English books printed by Caxton and will always have additional interest from having inspired Tennyson in his life work *Idyls of the King*.

The first Elizabethan age stirred British literature to a splendid brilliance. Even the Queen's schoolmaster was described by Thomas Carlyle as "one of the freshest, truest spirits one has met with; a scholar and a writer, yet a genuine man." Sir Walter Raleigh wrote his ambitious *History of the World* and his book was characteristic of the Elizabethans with their daring enterprise. English tragedy began with Sackville's *Gorboduc* and English comedy was launched with Udall's *Ralph Roister Doister* in 1566 and, of course, William Shakespeare was writing plays that were incomparable in their vigour, wit and sublime language.

The Restoration gave us Milton and Dryden after which there was an unhappy period in English writing. The 18th century was a more fertile field and produced a number of great works such as Gibbons' *Decline and Fall of the Roman Empire*. The French Revolution shattered conventional literary thinking and led to Coleridge considering a communistic scheme of a "Pantiocracy" to be founded on the banks of Susquehanna, but the idea was abandoned as Europe settled down again to government by the elite for the elite.

It is obvious in all this that English literature has been profoundly affected by both religion and politics but at the present day perhaps the major question dominating English literature is the titanic struggle between democratic thought, procedures, and methods of achievement, and those adopted by the Communist countries where the state is more important than the individual because, it is argued, that only the state can achieve security, work, and safety for the citizen. This great basic struggle has perhaps affected the theatre more than the world of books but it overshadows all the arts to an increasing degree.

Speaking in terms of the present day it will be of real benefit to the new author to familiarise himself with the whole field of English literature and, ideally, with American literature and European literature as well. If from a strictly practical point of view he wishes to know what is being successful in the world of books at any given moment, he cannot do better than visit bookshops and spend a morning browsing. He will then have acquainted himself with the kind of books which different publishers are currently accepting.

Connected with this whole question of the changing pattern of literature is the changing style of books, both their format and their contents, and this can only be realised by reading a book and comparing it with a similar book of a decade ago. Finally, each author will develop a style of his own. This is a child of his character, his personality, his own taste, his sensitivity to language and words and his natural habit of expression. Style cannot be invented or even dictated. It must come naturally. At its best it is highly individualistic and completely genuine. It can never be forced or contrived. It will always bear the stamp of the writer and incidentally reveal a great deal about him. It is a habit but a most indicative one and is only acquired by writing consistently over a period of time.

CHAPTER 13

Publicity — Promoting an Image

Authors divide themselves into the quiet ones who seldom make the headlines except in reviews — favourable or unfavourable — of their books, and those extrovert characters who use their books as a key to public life by lecturing, appearing on radio and television, and taking part in the big public debates that constantly erupt in the Letters to the Editor columns of the daily and weekly newspapers.

My own inclination was always to seek fun as well as profit from authorship and this I was able to do. Many authors and playwrights have achieved this. In the world of the theatre two young men gained fame, fortune and excitement by daring, extrovert originality when *Jesus Christ Superstar* exploded on to the stage as a British musical. *Evita* did the same thing. The young men connected with these spectacular and splendid shows became instant celebrities. A little fame — or notoriety — adds spice to life. Television in particular is a wonderful medium for "getting to know them". "I saw you on TV last night" lightens an author's day. He is often gregarious by nature and loves to be loved. If he cannot be loved, a little hate will do. But please, please do not ignore him.

When you write books for your livelihood, or to make up an inadequate income, you are in the tradition of men who for centuries have taken advantage of their independence and their articulate gifts to harangue or advise the public on every possible subject. They have published their diaries, they have written autobiographies pursuing their prejudices, they have dabbled in politics and, in general, have been licensed to say what they like, when they like, to whom they like. The Court Jester in times forgotten had a similar privilege. No-one could take offence at the Jester's offensive remarks. Only he was allowed to take a liberty — and he had absolute protection.

The modern author plays this role without jesting and

without privilege. He can be sued for libel or for slander, like everyone else, but in a world of the big conglomorates, political, social and international, he is the little free man who can still in Britain, in Europe and in most Commonwealth countries, as well as the United States, broadcast his views which will often run counter to the prevailing fashionable mood.

To achieve this kind of audience and publicity I have been discussing is especially valuable for the older man — or woman — who is entering the author's trade. If he has been submerged in some profession, such as the law, which forbids publicity or in a business where it is necessary to offend no-one, this newcomer will be entirely unknown to the public. Such was my case. I remedied this first of all by appearing on television in an interview with a charming creature then known — deferentially — as the First Lady of Television. I had written a book in which I suggested that frank polygamy in the Islamic tradition might be preferable to humbug in sex relations in Britain. This was before sex became promiscuous. Before appearing we had agreed that there would be no personalities. Towards the end of the programme she said: "I think you are the most conceited man I have ever met." I took this feminine remark as a compliment. Next day polygamy was all the rage in the less serious papers. My next step was to stand against Harold Wilson in Huyton and poll 3,600 votes for ten days campaigning. And finally, I incurred the wrath of many by running South African advertising for three years. When as a result of this experience I became convinced that "apartheid" was a "modern form of slavery" the South African Government erupted in angry accusation. I was condemned again.

Every author will make his choice either to be the quiet man or the extrovert or perhaps have it made for him by his nature. Nor is the choice absolute. The lecture tour, which is a serious and well organised business, will win you many friends and certainly help the sale of your books as well as bringing in a usually much needed cash flow.

The United States circuit tour is by far the best organised — and the most lucrative. America may be a young brash nation no longer, but the thirst for information and culture is still there. The tours are usually strenuous — the promoters have to make a profit — but if you are fit enough they are enjoyable. You are likely to receive delightful hospitality. On my first tour I attended chapel on Sunday at Vassar University as the only man present and the day was crowned by having one lovely girl to turn the pages of my hymn book while another did the same service for my prayer book. This was life as it should be lived...

In order to keep his name before the public an author is free to indulge in freelance journalism. His contribution will often arise out of the kind of books with which he is identified. For instance, an author who specialises in crime has an opportunity whenever some atrocious and bizarre murder hits the headlines or some gigantic fraud — preferably by city dignitaries — has shocked the public, if the public can react in this way any more.

In the course of a great criminal trial points will certainly arise that are food for journalism. If no comment is allowed during the trial, certainly there will be discussion after the sentences. Or the author may write a book on the crime itself. I had experience of this in the terrible Moors Murders case. I attended the trial and noted that the actor Emlyn Williams was also observing it in order to write an excellent book. I persuaded the then Bishop of Exeter to write my foreword, a modest step in one-up-manship. I thought mine was the better book, but my rival's sold more copies.

Opportunism is the soul and salt of journalism. When the King of Laos died suddenly no-one in Fleet Street knew anything about him. "Oriental absolute Lord of Life dies." Yes, but what kind of man was he? I had three offers to buy 1,500 words if delivered in time over the phone to make the next day's issue of the paper. We made it easily. So, if you think that this kind of foray into Fleet Street as a freelance journalist interests you, consult (again) your *Writers' and Artists' Year Book* and there under the heading "Newspapers and magazines" they all are complete with the necessary information and the editors' names. Very likely you will be approached or you may approach the news desk. Everyone is in a desperate hurry so you should be quick and decisive, especially about the fee which you will have confirmed in writing that day.

There has, for some time, been a feeling among journalists' Trade Unionists that the freelance author is trespassing on their preserves, but if the Society of Authors registers as a Trade Union this little difficulty — which has never been insuperable — will presumably vanish.

In any case, the public figure who has special standing or knowledge is sometimes essential to a newspaper. Recently, Mr Peter Hain, a well-known political figure, had an excellent article in the *Daily Telegraph* on the Russian dissidents. It gave a slant that the man with a purely Fleet Street background might not have had. Politicians are always in demand as occasional contributors, but so are authors who have made a particular subject their own.

Occasionally the "cheap end" of the book market may bring in substantial rewards and bring the author a wider circle of contacts. We wrote a book on the Profumo-Stephen Ward tragedy that sold "like hot cakes" as did the cheap paper back biography of Sir Winston Churchill. Never despise the paperback. It is the most stable market in the book business and money invested by the publisher brings a good return both for him and his author. I should not need to mention that the relevant information as to publishers who specialise in paperbacks is in the *Writers' and Artists' Year Book*.

The critics are said to build or destroy the reputation of authors. I do not think they do but a really good review by a critic of standing who has done his home work will help an author on his way. It is not true that all critics are disappointed authors. Many are men of culture and character and one should always read their reviews carefully, benefitting, if one can, from the criticism. If the criticism seems to be unfair one can steal an extra bow by pointing out factual inaccuracies which it is difficult for the paper concerned not to print. More — free — publicity. Sometimes just a few words will increase sales notably. The *New York Times* having said of *The Green Garuda*, "Sparrow writes with style and asperity", my sales in America nearly doubled.

Never resent criticism. After all, once you jump into the ring and write a book you are fair game for criticism. Never be hurt by what critics say. Anything may have happened. Perhaps the critic's wife may have left him that morning. He may have had a disastrous row with his Bank Manager. His son may have been arrested on a drunk and disorderly charge. Or, he may just be feeling very unwell. In a case when the critic has been obviously venemous or just beastly an urbane letter pointing out the injustice sometimes brings an apology — and a much kinder review of your next book. The author has to be something of a diplomat. So, file your reviews. They are the verdict of your peers. And it is no bad medicine to take a lesson in humility each time you re-read them, cherishing the nice ones and asking yourself the question, when perusing the ferocious ones, "Was I really as bad as all that?" And, if so — "Am I any better now?"

Many new authors will say to themselves: "Why should I ever become involved in a public or publicised life?" If they feel this, then surely they should not leave the ranks of the quiet authors who stand or fall by their books alone. This chapter is intended merely to point out the sidelines of the writing business that are open to the adventurous and to those whose confidence or conceit is so substantial that they enjoy the jousting of a society accustomed to giving its public figures a fairly rough time. This, of course, applies to the press as well. When they ring up, as surely they will, "No comment" is a callous and sometimes cruel answer. If possible, give them something to pin their piece on. And the publicity will not do you any harm unless, of course, for some reason they are hunting you. Then it is easy to be elusive. The chase will quickly end. And if the trouble is of real interest you can put them all into your next book....

Thus the choice is yours. A quiet life or the open forum? If you opt for the latter do not forget that you can fight battles for causes in which you believe, not only in your own country but overseas, world-wide. You are an author activist. That is my type of authorship, but my wife says: "Can't we have some peace for a few months?" I try to obey, not always with success.

Authors do not as a rule have rigid rules of morality. But I think that most of us try to avoid bringing our profession — and it is a profession first and a business second — into disrepute.

CHAPTER 14

The Summing-Up

New writers who have had the fortitude to read this book from start to finish will, I hope, escape a great deal of wasted time and many mistakes as they start out on a writing career. May I sum up the main points that I think are worth making a note of, points that are intended to be a guideline to keep the author out of trouble and ensure, as far as this is possible, success in the book business.

For convenience I have numbered them.

1. Choosing your line — often by a process of trial and error — is supremely important. A new writer who moves himself into a type of book he is unsuited, either by experience or by temperament, to write, suffers great frustration. So the advice is to get it right. No time spent in finding which type of book suits you is wasted. It is much future time saved.

2. The information in this book on "the tools of the trade" is based on long experience but each writer must choose for himself the tools with which he can work comfortably and efficiently.

3. The suggestions laid down for research and the synopsis technique are essential to writing a good orderly manuscript. The whole of an author's work should be conducted on orderly lines and if he has the relevant research and the synopsis at hand when he starts a book he is on the way to achieving a publishable book.

4. Publisher-Author relationship may make or mar an author. This is a special relationship if ever there was one. It is well worthwhile to understand the publisher's attitude, his motives and the critical and financial aspects that determine whether he will publish your book or not, and, even more important, whether you will become a recognised contributor to his List.

5. The chapter on Publisher's contracts is really at the core of the whole business. Authors too often "skim through" their contracts. This is or may be fatal. The author must know exactly what his commitments are in order that he may keep faith with his Publisher. The Publisher, because he draws up the contract with his lawyers, knows his obligations only too well. In nine cases out of ten he will be punctilious in observing the contractual terms.

6. Your variety of choice is so wide that new authors may find it valuable to have the scope of the choice indicated as it is in this chapter. New authors often write for years without realising how many opportunities there are for exploitation.

7. The chapter on films, TV and radio speaks for itself and as it was all founded on personal experience, and not on theory, it may be of real value.

8. The chapter on Agents, Copyright and Defamation which includes libel is meant to warn the new writer of the ever present dangers of libel and the disastrous consequences that sometimes follow its publication. In cases of danger developing, by all means consult a lawyer, but better still avoid it altogether by adopting the guidelines suggested here.

9. Foreign markets are very important and becoming increasingly so every year, that the new author needs to acquaint himself with these opportunities as soon as he starts his career.

10. Tourism. I have written more extensively on this comparatively new and fast growing aspect of the writing business because, having made a success of it, I am anxious that others should be in a position to achieve the kind of travel and pleasure that I obtained from it.

11. This chapter on publicity will not, I think, be found in other books on how to become a viable author. It may well be considered that the question of how private or how public an author becomes is a matter of his own choice. It is. But unless this aspect of an author's life is brought to his notice, the opportunities and rewards of publicity may never even occur to many whose extrovert natures should contribute to their success. After all, if we consider the author as a part of the

entertainment business, then it may be as necessary for him to be identified by the Public as it is for the actor and all entertainers. A rapport between the author and the public can do no harm and contacts are always potentially valuable. For this reason, fan mail should always be promptly and carefully answered.

12. Perhaps one of the most important chapters of the book indicates clearly the great amount of highly skilled work which the Publisher has to do to transform a manuscript into a marketable book. Unless the Author understands the full scope of this operation he will not be adequately informed on a major facet of the book business.

Finally, in this summing-up I have tried to bring all the strands together, hoping that they make a coherent and helpful pattern.

There is a myth that authors only write when "inspired", when in fact they write after careful thought and thorough research. As they write there is a certain lubrication and the pace quickens.

There is great pleasure to be gained from writing good books. One has a means of unique communication with the public and even with one's own and other countries. It is a privilege that should never be abused.

I do not know whether a majority of my fellow authors will agree with me, but I feel strongly that the author has an opportunity in his writings of strengthening the courage and confidence of his countrymen. Of course, such a message can only be conveyed if it arises naturally out of the text, but, if it does, it is of value to the nation.

One element I have not mentioned that is as important to the author as to the lawyer, the soldier or the worker without which hard work may bring slow rewards. It is, of course, *luck*. I wish you plenty of it.